LIGHTS ON!
A REFLECTIVE JOURNEY
Illuminations to Move Your Life Forward with Ease

CLAIRE KNOWLES

Lights On! and Lights On! Workshop©
www.LightsOnWorkshop.com
www.LightsOnLeadershipSuccess4Women.com

In association with Richard N. Knowles & Associates, Inc.
www.RNKnowlesAssociates.com

Yes, You Can Turn Your Lights On Too!

Claire E. F. Knowles
6083 Bahia del Mar Circle, # 564
St. Petersburg, FL 33715
1-716-622-7753
Claire@LightsOnLeadershipSuccess4Women.com (or)
CEFK1@aol.com
www.LightsOnLeadershipSuccess4Women.com
www.LightsOnWorkshop.com
www.RNKnowlesAssociates.com

Limits of Liability and Disclaimer of Warranty

The author and publisher shall not be liable for your misuse of this material. This book is strictly for informational and educational purposes.

Warning – Disclaimer

The purpose of this book is to educate and entertain. The author and/or publisher do not guarantee that anyone following these techniques, suggestions, tips, ideas, or strategies will become successful. The author and/or publisher shall have neither liability nor responsibility to anyone with respect to any loss or damage caused, or alleged to be caused, directly or indirectly, by the information contained in this book.

ISBN: 978-0-9721204-4-9

WHAT IS THIS BOOK ABOUT?

The author felt compelled to write *Lights On! A Reflective Journey* —originally as separate articles penned for various women's magazines and e-zines, and now as a compendium—to provide light markers for moving forward along life's pathways for both our personal and professional journeys.

Lights On! propels you forward. May these articles connect you with solid, heart-warming virtues and may your inner light flicker with renewed knowing. May you be emboldened with courage to face and embrace life's situations. In every single moment, you get to choose what you will think, what you will do, and how you will be.

These *Lights On!* sparklers will help you to find clarity and coherence as you travel your personal and professional paths. And if you are a leader working within the business world, you'll find the articles on women and leadership helpful for dealing with tangled workplace concerns. Yes, you can lift up the good and find coherent and courageous ways through the mire, with ease and with your *lights on* (if you want to!).

While the author draws from the good work of many others in the realm of "becoming better and better as we face and embrace life's situations," you'll find her unique perspectives refreshing.

So, hold the joyful expectation to have:
...a little time to catch your breath.
...an opportunity to change something if you want to.
...a chance to get back in touch with something if you want to.
...a moment of truth that is between only you and your inner self.
...the space to surprise yourself.
...the knowledge that you find and travel your own path.
...the opportunity to turn your lights on.

DEDICATION

This book is lovingly dedicated to my husband, Richard, the love of my life, and to my daughter, Christine, the joy of my life. It is also dedicated to my three wonderful stepdaughters, Beth, Dorothy, and Cynthia, who continue to openly embrace me into the family-fold. This book is written with women in mind, so this dedication fondly extends to my earliest teachers—my sisters, Vee and Paulie, and my late mother, Helen.

ACKNOWLEDGEMENTS

I extend a special "thank you" to all who have encouraged me to complete this book-writing project. In the article entitled "Unfinished Business" you'll note that this endeavor has been calling me to move forward. This Write a Book in a Weekend® project started during the throes of a surprise hospital stay and has continued over several months with strong encouragement from family, friends, and colleagues.

Thanks also to my women's network colleagues within WesternNewYorkWomen.com (www.WNYWomen.com), New York State Women, Inc., Zonta International, the Interfaith Council, Women Leaders, NAWBO, and the YWCA for your solid and continuous support of my work.

—Claire Knowles

ABOUT THE AUTHOR
Meet the Illuminator—Claire Knowles

Claire Knowles is an experienced, knowledgeable Human Resource Management professional. She approaches her work from a perspective of a deep belief in the goodness of people.

Her openness, honesty, and sense of fairness, combined with her instincts for what it takes to find the higher ground, has made her one of the most effective people in this field. In March 2000, she retired from the DuPont Company, where her professional career spanned 33 years and encompassed Human Resource Management and Labor Relations.

At DuPont, Claire was responsible for personnel relations; labor; industrial relations; safety; health and environmental issues; medical, wellness, and EAP programs; purchasing functions; overall site services; and community relations. One of her key functions was to help staff and leadership develop clarity in their thinking around the myriad issues they faced in the constantly changing world.

She has since transitioned to the role of Independent Coach and Leadership Consultant. She is also a full partner in R.N. Knowles & Associates, Inc. She currently assists individuals and organizations to collaboratively find clear paths of action to complete their work and personal goals, fully aligned with clear principles. She is a people person, a deep listener, and she uses the Living Systems approach to problem solving for personal and organizational change efforts.

Claire graduated from the State University of New York with a degree in Business Management and Economics. She majored in Human Resource Management and Labor Relations. In addition, she is certified in Mediation, a course recognized by the NY State Unified Court System. She is also an OSHA-certified safety training professional. Claire serves on the Board of Directors of The Center for Self-Organizing Leadership.

Claire is the creator of Lights On! and Lights On! Workshop©— especially for women: success workshops, speaking engagements, consulting, facilitation, presentations, retreats, coaching, and helping women's organizations and women-run businesses *become the best they can be.*

CONTENTS

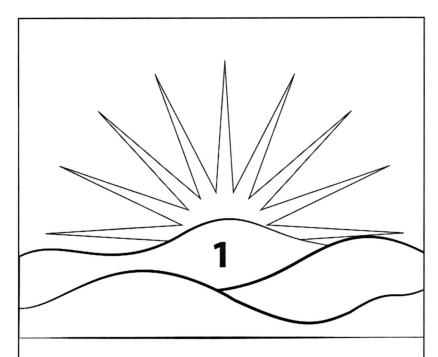

1

COLORFUL AND POWERFUL...

YES WE ARE!

Colorful Images...and Chocolate!

We've all had those times when we're "feeling blue." You've probably caught yourself saying, "I'm feeling a bit drab today." Most women understand this fully—this feeling comes when we just seem to need a little boost of optimism and a means to whisk that drab feeling away!

So how is your world looking today? Is today a day where you are in a vibrant mood—a "color me beautiful" mood? How illuminated are you today?

How do you lift your spirits when you feel a bit drab? I try to talk myself into a good mood. Mind over matter. Change my thoughts, and I can change my world. Think positive. Find something really exciting on which to focus. Be grateful. Sometimes I interrogate myself; I ask what is it that is behind this feeling? What is the root cause? And I keep asking that question until I can peg it. Once I name it, I can address it. Sometimes I go for a long walk. Physical exercise helps; so does fresh air and deep abdominal breathing. Each is uplifting in itself.

But the fastest way for me to lift up my spirits is with *chocolate!* Chocolate is a wonderful mood booster. Supposedly, chocolate stimulates the brain's dopamine production. Dopamine is important for diminishing pain sensations, enhancing pleasurable ones, and creating a sense of overall well-being. So there you have it—chocolate helps to create a sense of well-being. And when you possess a sense of well-being, you see the world in its full color spectrum. You become vibrant and animated!

Think about this. If I have a continual craving for chocolate, does that mean that I also have a continual desire for well-being? For happy moods? You bet. I'm addicted to life! Welcome to my colorful, chocolate-loving world.

God's Breath Is in This Somewhere!

I slept on the couch overnight—on purpose. I was experiencing one of those nasty colds, and my coughing and hacking were not something I wanted my husband to lose sleep over. So, off to the couch I went.

I awoke to a surprise in my changed setting. That cozy couch is in our living room where there are large windows with higher transoms. As I opened my eyes to greet the new day, I noticed the subdued daylight. It was a gray November morning. Across the transom windows I saw the gray clouds moving west to east against a sky with even more shades of gray. I was entranced. How long had it been since I'd watched the clouds float by like this? Since I'd actually sat still long enough to observe this wonder?

While everything was gray, did I feel gloomy? No. Tranquility permeated this watchful time. What was it about being drawn in to this continual movement of these clouds—with their forming and reforming—that seemed to fill me? Is it not a pattern for our lives: always in motion, always moving forward? I was attuned to the physical reality of the clouds moving by me, while I was simultaneously amazed at connecting into a deeper realm of my being. And this day had just begun!

My mind filled with many thoughts as I watched that scene continuously pass by the window panes. I thought about clouds, about wind, water vapor density, the jet stream, the lake effects from living by the Great Lakes, the atmosphere, the stratosphere—so many of the scientific elements underpinning what I was observing. Yet my sense of contentment still longed for something more, something richer, something with deeper meaning for this moment.

"God's breath is in this somewhere," I said to myself—a thought that seemed to come out of nowhere. That was it! My essential knowing for this moment!

What a delightful thought to start my day—thinking about God's breath. I took a deep breath. And another. This is going to be a wonderful, perfect day!

"Let yourself be silently drawn by the stronger pull of what you really love." ~Rumi

---

Mood Rings, and Why Your Life-Light Matters

Two very different thoughts and events converged for me yesterday.

One was about the mood ring and its varied colors and related meanings. I watched as two young adults tried on their new mood ring costume jewelry and shrieked and laughed as the color changed to reflect their respective emotions. One person's mood ring turned a dark blue color, supposedly indicative of happiness, love, passion, and romance; the other's turned amber color, indicative of nervousness, mixed emotions, being unsettled, and overall restlessness. Mood jewelry has been around for a long time. It is fun! I expect that you have worn a mood ring at some point in your life and, like these young women, also have had the experience of wondering if the mood ring would actually project your true emotions. Perhaps there is something to it—that your emotional level can be identified by the heat and tensions emerging from your own body.

I couldn't help but think about how wonderful it is to *not have to depend* on a mood ring to be the emotional barometer for our lives. As we mature, becoming more anchored in our own personal awareness—physically, emotionally, spiritually—we don't need mood rings to convey anxiety or well-being. We know where we stand. But wouldn't it be nice if mood rings could light up, like a beacon, every time we do something really good for another? Every time we are emotionally connected in service to others? Now that would be something!

There is a television advertisement where one person does a kind deed for a stranger, then that stranger for another, and the pattern of random acts of kindness keeps repeating, so that kindness becomes perpetual. How is it that we come to be in the right place at the right time to perform those certain acts of kindness, or to say just the right words at just the right time? Perhaps there is a greater orchestration of our lives at work here. Perhaps life's events intend moments of unique contact with other human beings—times wherein we are compelled to perform, times when our true light essence—our life-light—breaks through, and we choose only to "pay it forward."

Consider this: If I'm a beacon of light, I wonder what I'm projecting from moment to moment. Would my mood ring project that I'm ready to deliver my random act of kindness? To pay it forward? Am I ready to be in the right place at the right time and with the right words? If so, beam-me-up happy!

"Where am I meant to be shining? What have I been given with which to give?" ~Dawna Markova

Full Moon upon My Rising

It is glorious! It connects to my very core. It is inspiration extraordinaire!

Have you seen the full moon in the early morning?

There are times when something prompts me to rise early—especially when I'm in St. Pete Beach, Florida, at 5 a.m. I am awed by the full moon's glimmering reflection across the intercoastal waterway. It consumes me. Then, as the moon disappears into the horizon, and the sun's light takes over the skies, the day appears. The cycle is complete. Time moves on; the day moves forward.

I'd love to title this article "Full Moon Rising," but that would be flawed.

Technically, the moon I describe is setting. We know this pattern of lunar rise and set, and we appreciate the moon's dynamic dance with the sun. In this moment the moon is setting in wondrous splendor, rendering its capacity for perfection.

Beyond the observance is the inspiration that comes forth! What a great prescription for starting one's day beaming with joy and enthusiasm. How could one not have a good day? How could this invoke anything but happiness? How could one not feel "one with the universe"?

It was Abraham Lincoln who said, "I think a person is about as happy as he makes up his mind to be." This full moon, upon my rising, puts life into joyous perspective—I am happy to be here in this world, in this cycle of time. As the moon sets and the day begins, so does our call to begin again, to be even better than yesterday, to start anew. But there is something more—

deep inside I know that the wonder of the moon's setting is yet another marker for a day well-lived. Lights On!

Mashed Potato Clouds...A New Perspective

My daughter and I were traveling on an airplane when this wonderful story unfolded. At the time, she was about 6 years old. We were looking out the airplane's window at the clouds all layered below us. They were white, soft, pillow-like clouds—completely blanketing the view as far as we could see.

As we looked down on this splendor, I said in my motherly, thought-leading way, "Doesn't it look different from up here?" With much excitement, my daughter said, "Yes." Then she quickly added, "They look like fluffy mashed potatoes. It looks like a big ocean of mashed potatoes. And there's enough here to feed the whole world forever!"

What a wonderful thought, I noted to myself. I was so proud of my daughter's clear optimism, her happy childlike imagination, and her generous spirit.

Our conversation continued, of course, and we talked about lots of possibilities. My daughter also asked if I thought we might even see Mary Poppins popping through these clouds holding her umbrella—perhaps on her way to spark some happiness in a new family setting.

Next to us, seated in the aisle seat, was a rather stern-looking woman who had overheard our conversation about the clouds. Glumly, she said, "Those clouds are deceptive; they are white only on the top. They are dark rain clouds on the bottom, closer to the ground." Then she began to complain about rain, about too much rain, about her roof leaking, and about the storms this season.

All I could think was *what a way to spoil a moment*. But my daughter, who was generally shy, surprised me with "the last word." She looked directly at this woman and said, "The clouds are staying pretty up here for us, just like nice mashed potatoes, and there's enough for everybody—for you, too!" As she said this, she gave the woman her best smile, having absolute certainty in her words. The woman just nodded, and slowly smiled too; she said nothing further.

I was reminded in that moment how, when we come from our higher place, we not only raise ourselves up, we raise those around us.

Hooray for my daughter as she brought forth wisdom and abundance from a higher, positive, beautiful, mashed-potato place.

"Remember, You Are Not That Sharp Today!"

Whew! My husband spoke these words to me as I was about to go out the door to drive to the post office. I knew exactly what he meant. I'd been recovering from a surgical procedure, and I was about to operate a motor vehicle. He was simply reminding me that I needed to be extra cautious at this juncture—my first time behind the wheel since the surgery. At this point in my recovery, there were no driving restrictions; still, the admonition was worth noting.

Though I fully accepted this statement on the level at which it was intended, I caught myself pondering different meanings to those words. Do I hold expectations that I am razor-sharp? Sharp as a tack? Laser-focused? When am I not "sharp as ever"?

I went deeper inside my pondering—to when I first awaken from deep slumber. Each morning there is that split second when I have to "find myself" again. Who am I? Where am I? How am I in relation to my body and my environment? Oh yes, my everyday, precise, awakening-point-of-awareness tells me my name (the person for whom I answer). I awaken to my "self-identification." With all the traveling I do, it is not unusual to awaken, simultaneously becoming aware of the room in which my body happens to be and in which direction I'll find the bathroom! Yes, my awareness extends to my awakening body. Am I stiff? Do I need to stretch? I conclude that my daily *upon-awakening-process* is the *awareness point of life*—of coming into consciousness—of reclaiming my razor sharpness!

I'm reminded of that philosophical statement proposed by René Descartes, "I think, therefore I am." The simple meaning of the phrase is that someone wondering whether or not he or she exists is, in and of itself, proof that he or she does exist—at the very least, there must be an "I" who does the thinking.

Enough already! I am awake. I am conscious. I am sharp as ever! I awoke this morning—and came into consciousness, into full awareness. I exist. I know who I am, where I am, and how I am! I'm as sharp as ever! I'm ready to get behind this wheel; I've got places to go, things to do. I am sharp! A little reminder doesn't hurt, though!

Unfinished Business

It seemed very strange. A male red cardinal had been bumping into our windows, which face the woods, for over a year and a half. At first, we thought that because it was nesting season, perhaps this cardinal was seeing his reflection in our windows and was just being territorial. But his bumping (flying up to the window, and then banging it with his feet and beak) continued—over and over again, season after season.

We tried to ignore it. At times, this bumping occurred up to a dozen times in an hour. One day we were sitting at our kitchen table with our insurance agent; while we'd learned to disregard it, our agent was fascinated. He questioned why this cardinal would continue to bump into our windows like that—he found it very distracting. We couldn't tell him why. Indeed, it was a strange phenomenon. Our neighbors, also with windows backing up to the woods, had *not* experienced the intrigue of this beautiful-yet-persistent cardinal.

My husband and I wondered, often aloud: What is this colorful bird trying to tell us? Is there a message he is trying to deliver? It was at this juncture that I researched information on the symbolism and meaning of the cardinal totem. The cardinal, with his standout crimson color, is considered a messenger of the air. He is bold and confident. Known by his loud whistle-like call, he demands attention, urging us to hear what is carried through the air—the message on the wind. When a cardinal appears in your life, it is time to pay attention. Native Americans view the visit of a cardinal as delivering the message *to become acutely aware that you have unfinished business to which you must attend.* In addition, the male cardinal carries dual messages of *persistence*, and also of *confidence/self-worth/self-importance.* The underlying message is that the repetitive appearance of the male cardinal in your path is about coming to recognize one's own self-worth, one's own self-importance, and, accordingly, to experience a renewed vitality, moving forward boldly and confidently, with persistence, to conclude what is unfinished business for you. Yes, the visit of the cardinal is intended to motivate us to *get on with it!*

Shortly after that, my husband and I met with our estate attorney to complete our wills and estate plans. As we have a blended family, it is important that this be complete, for obvious reasons. Interestingly, with that concluded, the pesky cardinal suddenly became absent from his window-knocking. We'd completed that unfinished business. We actually missed his visits! We wondered if something dire had happened to him.

Next, we were absent from our home, as we decided to winter in Florida. When we returned in the late spring, happily, so did our red companion. He came knocking again! But the pattern of his visits to our windows changed. Now his knocking was much less frequent and only when I was in that area of the house (not when my husband was present). So, in what area of life am I supposed to be paying more attention?

I know that I have some unfinished business. I know that I have certain work that I am supposed to complete, that requires persistence, and that hinges on self-worth and self-importance— not in a puffed-up way, but rather, because I have writing to do that comes from within, from my own life experience and from my heart. It must be brought forth and conveyed. It compels me forward; I mentor through my writing. One of my life's lessons includes *getting on with things—to just do it!* Thus, my writing continues.

Each of us has unfinished business. You, like me, were created to make a positive difference in this world—to impact our society in some positive way, to make the world a better place, to step forward with your gifts, and to do what you can.

We all can benefit from a visit from the cardinal. Renewing our vitality, recognizing our self-worth, honoring the self-importance of our own being, strengthening our persistence for completing those intended endeavors—that's all good. And we can each benefit from some nudging along the way.

Thank you, Mr. Red! I appreciate your nudging me forward (again)!

"Every small, positive change we can make in ourselves repays us in confidence in the future." ~Alice Walker

I Just *Love* Your Shoes!

There is a children's book, *My Shoes Take Me Everywhere I Want to Go* by Marianne Richmond, that recently caught my attention. I was in the grocery store checkout line and was contemplating what to speak about at an upcoming presentation to a gathering of professional women. And there it was...the idea emerged!

The storyline of this delightful book is told from the perspective of a child. The child shares that her mother had told her that she essentially was born without any clothes. In fact, all the parts of her were bare—her head, her feet, even her toes. But that condition changed very quickly because now she has shoes that take her everywhere—everywhere she wants to go! She has dancing shoes, tennis shoes, and sandals for the beach. She has shoes for school. She has running shoes and princess shoes, flip-flops and party shoes. Her shoes provide her journey after journey. All she has to do is don her favorite pair of shoes and they take her everywhere—everywhere she wants to go!

Let's extrapolate this story from the little girl in each of you to the multi-dimensional adult career woman! Let's peek at the many shoes that are in your life closet that take you everywhere you want to go:

- Are your shoes carrying you to the places you want and need to go?

- To the milestone places along your intended life path?

- To the places that nurture your personal growth and development?

Every pair of shoes that you don says something about some aspect of your essential nature. They represent you in many ways, and

17

they participate fully in your journey. They carry you everywhere you want to go. And *you* are the manager of *your* life shoe closet! Are you nurturing all those aspects of your essence? Are some of your "me-shoes" taken for granted? Neglected or taking a back seat to other priorities? Have you forgotten how powerful and beautiful you are in *all* the dimensions of your life—in *all* the shoes that you wear? Your shoes are dedicated to the art of your well-being—professionally, personally, recreationally, and spiritually. They reflect your personal being in all aspects of your life. Here's to celebrating the aspects of you reflected in all of your shoes, wherever they are carrying you, and to celebrating the "me-shoes" that grace your entire life closet.

As the manager of your life's shoe closet, here are some pertinent questions:

- Have you been neglecting some shoes in your life closet lately?

- Are there some that you are wearing out? Or others you just haven't found time to wear?

- When was the last time you had your sneakers on and took a good walk—because you needed it for life balance?

- When was the last time you took the time to walk the beach in your sandals? Or maybe in bare feet?

- When was the last time you spent the whole day in your slippers—because you needed that?

- When was the last time you had on your dancing shoes? Or your Mary Janes?

- Have you taken inventory lately of all the shoes that adorn the full spectrum of your life? How are you caring for their well-being?

- What shoes are you choosing to carry you to where you want to go next? Where is that?

The next time you open your life shoe closet to choose the right pair of shoes, you just might hear, "Hey, pick me, pick me—wear me today!" Because your "me-shoes" want to take you wherever it is that you *want* to go. If you are really, really listening to the inner teacher in you, you'll know that those shoes that are crying out, "Hey, pick me, pick me—wear me today!" are likely the ones that will also take you to where you *need* to go.

So off you go! The shoes you've chosen are taking you on new adventures, new journeys.

And, oh, by the way—I just *love* your shoes!

Note: A version of this article by Claire Knowles originally appeared in NIKE *online magazine, New York State Women, Inc, Spring 2010.*

I Am a Butterfly!

My life story is about emergence—real life transitions—that always move me forward and provide me with opportunities to flutter my wings and fly!

I promise myself...

...To be so strong that nothing can disturb my peace of mind.

...To talk health, happiness, and prosperity to every person I meet.

...To make all my friends feel that there is something in them.

...To look at the sunny side of everything and make my optimism come true.

...To think only of the best, to work only for the best, and to expect only the best.

...To be just as enthusiastic about the success of others as I am about my own success.

...To forget the mistakes of the past and press on to the greater achievements of the future.

...To wear a cheerful countenance at all times and give every living creature I meet...a smile!

...To give so much time to the improvement of myself that I have no time to criticize others.

...To be too large for worry, too noble for anger, too strong for fear, and too happy to permit the presence of trouble.

...To think well of myself and to proclaim this fact to the world, not in loud words but in great deeds.

...To live in the faith that the whole world is on my side—so long as I am true to the best that is in me.

Adapted from "The Optimist Creed," first published in 1912 in C.D. Larson's book, *Your Forces and How to Use Them.* A shortened version is used today by Optimist International, a worldwide group of people who are focused on making a positive difference in their lives and in the world.

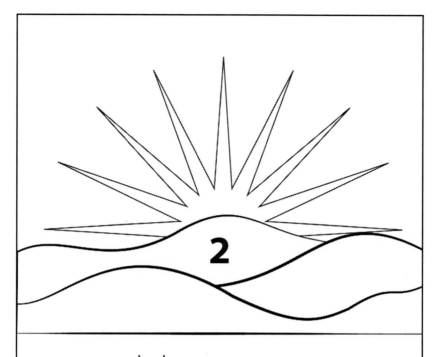

2

MOVING
FORWARD

If You Don't Know Where You're Going, You'll Probably End Up Somewhere Else

The above phrase is actually the title of a book written in 1974 by David Campbell, PhD (Argus Communications). I was browsing through a wonderful used book sale in Ithaca, NY, and the book practically jumped off the shelf at me. As a coach and consultant I recognize that this title is profound.

Each of us is on the road to somewhere. Unless you know what you want from life, you are not likely to stumble across it. But how do you know what you want? Especially when you are young and still not quite certain what life is all about—how do you decide? Or what happens when you are at a crossroads? What compels you forward? What repels you backward? Can you find the stillness to truly listen to your inner guidance—to your intuitive self? Can you visualize a path forward?

Without a vision, a target, and goals, you are rambling; you're without focus. Think of looking through a pair of binoculars. If the lens is clouded, you can't see where you are going—you are hit and miss. The clearer the view you have of your target, the better your ability to focus, the better your intuitiveness can emerge, and the more that the synchronicity of the universe can rally to help you reach it.

For example, President Kennedy created a vision and mantra for the US in 1961, after Russia's Sputnik rattled our confidence. He stood up and said that America will put a man on the moon by the end of this decade and will return him safely to earth. Even the best scientific minds of the day didn't know if that was possible. He created a positive target. He made a declaration. He made a choice. He declared the vision and said yes to it. And America rallied. We cannot underestimate the power of vision, declaration, and choice. And what happened? NASA and America did it. Neil Armstrong, 1969. The collective vision was manifest.

You co-create your own future too. Will your future be determined by circumstances beyond your control? Will you drift through life, or will you play an important role in determining its force and direction? This depends on whether your binoculars have their lens caps still on and it depends on whether the lenses are clear. What doors have you closed? What doors are still open to you? The more talents you develop, the more skills you acquire, the more doorways to opportunity can be opened. Can you see your way?

Are your Lights On? Are your binoculars providing you great focus? Can you see your target? Can you envision the steps to get you there? Lights On!

"Drifting through life without aim or purpose is the first cause of failure." ~Napoleon Hill

---

It Is What It Is—Period

It **is what it is.** There are things that are not within our power to change.

This phrase is one that I tell myself sometimes and tell others I coach. Usually it is stated in concert with difficult situations, beyond one's control, clearly outside one's sphere of influence. Sometimes having the courage to speak up, to say what needs to be said when it needs to be said and in a way that it needs to be said, is most appropriate. Some conflicts call for action. Sometimes you are the person who needs to intercede. Sometimes the elephants hiding under the rug need to be uncovered and constructively addressed. Sometimes it is your role to right a situation, to improve it for the better. Sometimes the conversation that needs to be held has your name written on it. Sometimes the action required is yours to take. Sometimes situations call for courage and taking principled measures. Sometimes you must step forward.

Sometimes, though, the decision to let it go, and to let things be is the wiser choice. Here are several sources for this wisdom:

First, the Serenity Prayer:

"God, grant me the serenity to accept the things I cannot change, the courage to change the things I can, and the wisdom to know the difference."

Accepting things one cannot change does not mean condoning those things. (People often lose this perspective.) It means accepting that some things are not yours to change, and are not your battle to fight. Some things are not yours to control, nor should you invest your energy or time into them. But rather, you should put your focus, energy, and attention elsewhere—on the important things where you can make a difference.

Second, the Universal Law of Allowing:

The Universal Law of Allowing requires granting to others the same rights you ask for yourself—the right to be, have, and do what you choose. When you have an emotional reaction to someone else's behavior, stop and tell yourself: "This person is neither good nor bad. I neither like this person nor dislike this person. This person just is. This person is another human being doing the best this person can…given this person's conditioning, beliefs, circumstances, experiences, and present perceived needs." So, removing the emotional judgment of the person or the circumstance, my question then becomes: *"What aspect, if any, do I have within my gifts, talents, skills, knowledge, and experience to constructively offer this moment to make it better?"*

The bottom line: It is not what happens to us in life, but rather how we respond to it, that matters most. We choose our response. Sometimes we are respons-able. Sometimes it is our responsibility. Sometimes it is not. Sometimes we can make a difference. Sometimes we cannot. Sometimes our voice and our action would improve the situation, sometimes not. Sometimes we've already done all that we can. Sometimes our choice needs to be *to just let it be, because it is what it is, period!* Lights On!

Most Times Life Moves You Forward, But What Do You Do When It Doesn't?

"If you don't go after what you want, you'll never have it.
If you don't ask, the answer is always no.
If you don't step forward, you're always in the same place."
~Nora Roberts

Sometimes in my coaching I meet women who are stuck in their jobs or in difficult situations but who do not have the courage or the wherewithal to move on, women who know that something is deeply missing in their careers, or their relationships, or their lives, but can't bear to face it head-on. They can't lift up the essential conversation; they won't make the attempt to move things forward. Some are afraid of what others might think of them if they pursued a different direction.

Sometimes a woman is comfortable only in "venting"—in sharing her situation. She actually pushes back at any suggestions for moving forward; she finds more reasons for not taking action than she does for taking action. I've met women who just want to have the universe make their moves for them—waiting to be sucked into an ultimate change in circumstances, like being pulled down a river in white-water rapids, thus not having to initiate change for themselves.

I recall one woman who concluded that she would endure her marriage situation (being non-valued, verbally abused, and continually treated like a non-person) for whatever time it took her to outlive her husband, and then, when that day came, she'd be free to live her life in a meaningful way. While certainly it was that woman's personal decision, still it is a sad, sad commentary on being stuck. This same person, on a daily basis, chooses to

29

escape into a different world—a world of Harlequin romance. It is a daily daydream fantasy session that provides her with a temporary escape, an alternative, a make-believe way to be valued as a person—a survival mechanism. It doesn't have to be that way.

I've talked with women who, at one level, know what they need to do, know the conversation that is overdue, know the relationship that needs to be addressed, know the career they should pursue, know the resources they should seek, know the change they need to initiate, but they cannot move—they are paralyzed in place. I call this chrysalis paralysis—being stuck in one's own cocoon! This paralysis is one where it is perceived as more painful to have to initiate a change than it is to maintain the status quo. It is clearly a trap—a trap that is not what one wants, but is nonetheless more comfortable than the perceived alternative. Given a lack of courage, it is the best they can muster for the time being.

How do you break out of your comfort arena and make changes when life isn't moving you forward? Some basic questions to ask yourself are these:

- What would you do if you had the means? If you weren't afraid? If you had the money?

- What would you do if you had the wherewithal to do it? (If you couldn't do the first thing, then what would the next thing be to move you forward?)

- What is really stopping you from moving forward? What is the root of the stagnation? How can you overcome those barriers? Have you asked for any help? What baby steps forward could you take?

- Consider the playground spinner—the merry-go-round. Once you are on it, it is entirely up to you to *choose* when you are going to get off. You decide when you must get off—when you've had enough! Are you going to stay with the spinning...round and round and round? For how long?

- Whose permission do you think you need to make this change?

- Think about a forward timeline. If you do nothing to change this, how will this situation be different 1 year from now or 3 years from now? 5 years? 10 years? Even 20 years?

- If there's a conversation that is overdue and has your name on it, when will you speak up? Why does this have your name on it? What are you waiting for?

So, is life moving you forward? Or are you at a place where you need to break out of your comfort arena and make some changes? Are you waiting for Life? Or is Life waiting for you?

Recommended reading: If you are stuck and are spinning on that playground merry-go-round, Judith Sills' book, The Comfort Trap, or What If You're Riding a Dead Horse *is a must-read! "Face it," she says, "the horse is dead, and it is time to get off!"*

Life Transitions

"The Lesson: When we are ready to make a beginning, we will shortly find an opportunity!" ~William Bridges, Transitions

Our lives are filled with transitions. An example is transitioning from infant to toddler to youngster to teenager to young adult to middle adulthood through to our end-life maturing. Within each of these "life stages," though, are the personal stories of many other important transitions. Each person's various chapters have *endings, transitions,* and *new beginnings*. Some may involve family situations, relationships, career situations, health situations, education paths, with integral combinations and complexities therein. All these various transitions can essentially be modeled—or patterned— along the lines of *endings, transitions,* and *new beginnings.* My husband once remarked as he thought about our blended family with children and grandchildren across various age ranges, "We always have somebody in transition!"

With this *endings/transitions/new beginnings* model or pattern we can identify where we are at a given point in time. We can also cope better with the difficult, painful, or confusing times of our lives.

So what happens when an ending is about to happen? William Bridges, an authority on transitions, shares that there are three Ds that provide the signals to us. When we listen to our intuitive voice, we will sense one or more of these:

Disengagement – When you find yourself being disengaged whether willingly or unwillingly from the activities, relationships, settings, or roles that have been important to you, you get signals of a time of personal transition. Feeling like you don't fit in is a common, recognizable theme. There's often a nudging to let go.

Dis-identification – Not being quite sure of who you are, or what you are, or where you belong anymore—particularly in identifying with a job or career. It is the breaking of old connections and self-definition. It is feeling like a nonentity.

Disenchantment – This encompasses a long list of feelings, from disillusionment to betrayal. It is when you feel cheated, victimized, repelled, discouraged, or largely diminished. Sometimes you're propelled forward because to stay is difficult too, and you reach the bifurcation point signaling that it is time to end, and to transition to something new, something different, something that feeds you.

So once we recognize the three Ds as happening, what can we expect next? Endings!

Endings: Sometimes the source of an *ending* can be evoked (come from within)—a gradual dawning as we learn from experience that what we are doing is not working and something needs to change. It can be provoked (come externally)—by means of the "pink slip." We need to recognize *endings* as opportunities—as well as losses. We should recognize (even celebrate) an *ending* with a ritual (a closure). It is best if a closure happens in a way that reflects upon and closes out the past, while providing a genuine openness for new directions to come.

Transitions: Then we come to *transitions*. This is the time that is exemplified by being "stuck." We are in neutral, not going forward, not going backward, treading water, paralyzed, waiting for clarity. This is when we need to take the time to listen to our inner teacher, to access our intuitive voice. It is the time to factually weigh things, to use both the rational mind and the intuitive mind. It is time to explore new options. When we are ready to move on, to make a new beginning, we will shortly find an opportunity! Sometimes we can be stuck in neutral—afraid to move forward, unwilling to go backward for a long, long time! In a transition we feel disconnected from the past, yet emotionally unconnected to the present, and unclear about the future. It is a place of ambiguity and not knowing. It is a place of churning. It is wise to use this time to reflect and get reoriented. I liken this transition place to being inside the cauldron of change—where things keep swirling until we're ready to move forward to a new place.

New Beginnings: Beginnings are like a new fern leaf starting to unfurl—opening to the world. *Beginnings* signify the launching of new priorities and a new direction. We receive the signal—a faint intimation of something different: a new theme, new insight, a new calling, an inner idea that keeps resonating. We are nudged forward. Something seems to excite. We might even have "the flash" of an intuitive sense of knowing. We find a renewed energy and a sense of being drawn to something new. We start forward.

Transitions form the basic pattern of our lives. At a deep level we know that these patterns are present. Intuitively we know. We can lift them up to understand what is happening. We have the knowledge of the three Ds, so we know what to be watchful for. Yes, we move on—life calls us to that action. We've transitioned—for now—to a new place. That's the wonder of life…transitions keep happening. It is by moving through ongoing life transitions that we discover pearls of wisdom, greater insight, and the opening to the next new growth possibility. Lights On!

*Recommended reading: This article is about life transitions. Two books by William Bridges (*Transitions *and* Managing Transitions, *Perseus Books, 1980 and 1991, respectively) are important to this topic and are highly recommended additions to your library. This article draws extensively from them.*

Moving Forward: Conscious of Our Choice of Words

Our busy days unfold like the Page-a-Day calendar that quickly melds into weeks, months, and years. As time flitters by, we internally crave meaning and fulfillment in our lives—hoping that we won't look back someday and regretfully say, "Is that all there is?" or "Success...but at what cost?"

Deep in our hearts we know that we are the managers of our own lives. Solely responsible! Dr. Phil frequently affirms this self-knowledge. So how can we best affect outcomes throughout our lives?

There are many self-help books for improving and transforming our lives. Yet we all know people who already have it together—who have mastered filling their lives with what matters most. You can master this as well! Personal (life) mastery goes beyond competence and skills. It means approaching one's individual life as a creative work—living life from a creative, positive, and proactive viewpoint, as opposed to a reactive one. It is being able to work with the forces of change, not resisting them. This requires some personal work. It means thinking positive and integrating into our personal and professional roles those daily, weekly, monthly, and yearly goals that are rooted in our identified core values. Core values act as our anchors—essential to maintaining meaning and purpose in our lives through all of the many life roles we play.

So, from the life-manager responsibility standpoint, have you actually taken the deeper personal insight time to honor and lift up your personal core values? And have you then decided how you want to have these core values show up in the various roles you play, day in and day out? Have you scheduled into your calendars or planners that which matters most?

The title of the popular self-help book by Dawna Markova, *I Will Not Die an Unlived Life*, sums it up—we need to live fully! We can start today—at this juncture and date on our personal Page-a-Day calendar. It can start simply with accepting personal responsibility *for the choice of words we use!*

Immediately, we can begin to use *conscious creative language* to effect positive outcomes in our lives! Conscious means to be fully aware: to be deliberate, intentional. Creative is proactivity in the making: to bring into being. We can take the initiative by using words that come out of our mouths to actually act in advance, rather than simply reacting to circumstances and events. By consciously choosing the words we say, we can further empower ourselves.

Here are some examples:

- Eliminate indifference. The next time you're asked what or where you want to do or go, be definitive. Never say, "I don't know; it doesn't matter." It does matter. With indifference in your language, you give your power away. Instead, be empowering...choose!

- Eliminate *problem* from your vocabulary. Replace it with *challenge*. As soon as you do that, the negativity associated with the problem is replaced with a positive array of ways and means to rise to the challenge. (It is human nature!)

- No more *buts*. *But* is a word of cancellation. It negates everything that was said before it. "I love your new dress... but why are you wearing those shoes?" If you have to use *but,* don't even bother to say anything. *But* translates into the negative.

- Eliminate the word *want*. Instead, use the word *choose*. When you use the word *want*, you essentially keep yourself in a state of *wanting*. (I *want* a better job; I *want* a better relationship; I *want* to lose weight. *Want* translates to a continual state of *wanting*!). Instead, *choose*. (I *choose* to have a better job; I *choose* to have a better relationship; I *choose* to be thinner; I *choose* to be healthy.) Once you deliberately *choose,* your awareness will begin to notice and beckon all the things that are necessary for you to move forward. You begin to deliberately create the future consistent with your choice. Once you've chosen, your future vision kicks in—it is like looking through a pair of binoculars; if the lens cover is on, you cannot see anything. You are blind. With a clear view, however, and your choice in focus, you now have a target for positively moving toward.

- Deliberately and consciously build these words into your language: I choose. I can. I am. I will. I have. I love. I create. I will enjoy. These are positive, forward-moving words. Next, give yourself permission to do the very thing your words endorse, that is, to choose, to do, to be, to have, to create, to love, to enjoy. The more you use these positive words (and conversely, avoid their negative opposites), the more you'll find that your proactive words will positively lift you up and move you forward.

- Work at consciously and deliberately developing this positive practice. Remember, *you* are the manager of your life and solely responsible for how it plays out—so use this conscious creative language process to positively influence your life outcomes.

As ye think, so shall ye be.

Note: This article was originally published in NIKE *online magazine, New York State Women, Inc., December 2009, by Claire Knowles. This version differs slightly from the original.*

Moving Forward: When You're Stuck

Sometimes you get stuck. As I coach people, I often share that it is perfectly fine to be "stuck in one's own cocoon" for a while. You need time to wallow, time to sort things out, time to rationalize, time to weigh the options, time to recover, and time to seek nourishment from within. Sometimes it is just a matter of getting really clear on what one's question or dilemma is all about. Can you name what is at stake? Can you share your emotion around the issue? Can you describe it fully?

Sometimes we need to put the universe (God, your creator, your source) on assignment to provide some direction, to provide a clear answer. Then, once the question has been voiced aloud, we need to stay alert and pay attention. Listen carefully to what your intuition (your inner teacher) tells you. What signs and signals do you *see or hear* that indicate options or directions? In what direction are you being compelled to move? It is encouraging to look and listen for answers everywhere—to notice what kinds of answers show up through people, chance comments, personal study, books, meditations, events, dreams, or intuitive knowing—that "flash of brilliance."

A number of years ago, I attended an intuition-based workshop called "Navigating the Soul's Journey," presented by Christine Page, MD. I was contemplating what I should do with Lights On! Workshop© as a business in the future. Should I discontinue it? Or should I put more effort into making it a stronger business? Or should I continue just as I was doing—working at it part-time—while I worked with my husband in two other business ventures? I asked the universe to please give me guidance for the right strategy at this juncture in my work life. I had been feeling pulled in multiple directions, trying to work at all three businesses and not convinced that I was making sufficient progress in any of them; things seemed so fragmented. I was hoping to come away with a priority for the investment of my time and effort, and I was not fully sensing the personal potency return that I needed.

My question was, "Should I continue to put my efforts into Lights On! Workshop©, including Lights On! Coaching?" Per instructions given at this conference, we were asked to find a quiet spot and to ask our question, then to spend the next hour just being quiet and alone, while walking around the hotel and the hotel grounds (where this conference was held). Specifically, we were to pay attention to what insights came forth.

As I walked around, I noticed the three huge, crystal chandeliers in the elegant hotel lobby, but from the mezzanine's close-up view I was taken aback. What I noticed was how many individual chandelier lights were burned out. I was struck by their number.

The thought that immediately came to me was: *these burned-out lights each need to be turned on.* The answer was suddenly very clear to me. My insight was that I needed to continue Lights On! work even if it was only one light at a time. And I also knew that this work was in addition to the work that my husband and I are called to do together—the other two businesses—because there were three big chandeliers hanging in a row. Interesting! For me, it certainly was what I needed at that time to move forward! So, as you ask your open questions, may you look and listen carefully and glean some important insights to move you forward too.

Postscript: I'm still involved with three businesses. The prioritization of my time and effort remains a doable dance. Each feeds my need for productive work, income, and contributing my wisdom gifts to this world. I'm so glad that I did not choose to dissolve Lights On! It has been a wonderful connection for me to women, women's groups, women's networks, and women-owned businesses.

Recommended reading: Carol Adrienne's book, When Life Changes or You Wish It Would *(2002, Harper Collins).*

Moving Forward: Full Potential Ahead!

"In the long run, we shape our lives, and we shape ourselves. The process never ends until we die. And the choices we make are ultimately our own responsibility." ~Eleanor Roosevelt

I'm naturally an optimist, so moving forward—engaging with the flow of life—makes good sense to me. I also hold high expectations. Why not expect the best? Why not be the best you can be? Why not choose wisely? Why not keep expanding?

I grew up on a dairy and grain farm. My dad, a man of undeniable down-home wisdom, used to say, "There's no use crying over spilt milk," meaning whatever has happened is behind you; you can't undo it, so move forward. I can still hear him say, "Don't whine; stop complaining. Just decide what you're going to do next, and then follow through—do it. Be expectant that things can change for the better, if you want them to change." Then he'd be silent for a long while, as I pondered my plight. The next probing question always came, "How do you want this to turn out?" And then he'd say, "So what are you going to have to do about this?" For him, teaching moments like these were about choosing to be a victim, *or* choosing to be the victor. Ultimately, my choice would decide the outcome.

My dad was teaching me to realize that the problems of life will always be there, and if I choose to accept them, own them, and take responsibility for them, then they quickly become new opportunities to grow, to learn, to become. And though he did not use this language, the meaning behind his words was also there—that through my choices, I co-create my own future.

Much has been written about the Universal Laws, and, in particular, about the Universal Law of Attraction. The Law of

Attraction is essentially a gift, available to all—a gift that helps us to keep moving forward, fully living our potential, *if we choose.*

Why is it important? Because each of us co-creates our own personal journey. Your thoughts, decisions, and choices today impact your tomorrows. What you say, what you think, and what you choose really do matter. Life agrees with everything you think, say, and believe. What you fill your mind with—your life is full of. You attract into your life what you think about. Life agrees with you and will show you just how right you are! There is power in your expectations, your thoughts, your words, and, of course, in your choices and your follow-through actions. So why not set high expectations—think them, dream them, speak them, and live them?

It is exciting, really—that there is co-creative power in setting and holding clear intentions. Forget wishful thinking—this is about intentionally shifting your conscious awareness up a notch! As ye think, so shall ye be!

Start by paying attention to your thoughts and words. Are you complaining? Bemoaning your plight? Belittling others? Are you saying, "I hate this _____?" Are you, by your own words, inviting more chaos and disharmony? More struggle? More problems? Are you able to step back and clearly put out to the universe (and prepared to diligently repeat) the very positive thoughts that invite and co-create a better tomorrow? Are you ready to flip things upside down—first, to find the positive in what you already have, and then to invite more of that into your life? Can you actually see what you want your future to look like? Do you know how you want things to turn out? Have you developed your roadmap? What are you choosing to do next?

Thanks, Dad, for planting those early seeds in me! Yes, new choices keep "sprouting" before me—and I know that every choice matters!

Recommended reading: In his book, Your Best Life Now *(2004, Warner-Faith), Joel Osteen speaks to moving forward with intention. He writes about the important steps for living at your full potential, including: "speaking life-changing words," "enlarging your vision," "raising your level of expectancy," and "choosing the right thoughts."*

Recommended listening: Dr. Wayne W. Dyer's audio book, The Power of Intention...Learning to Co-create Your World, *(2004, Hay House) shares research into intentions as an energetic force in the universe that allows the act of creation to take place. This work explores intention—not as something you do, but as an energy of which you are already a part, to which you are already connected.*

What Am I Coping With? Why?

"Problems are not the problem; coping is the problem."
~Virginia Satir

I'm writing this from 30,000 feet in the air. I'm on an airplane, sitting next to my hubby, on a four-hour flight from Vancouver to Houston. This will be directly followed by another flight—home!

So I have time to think—captive time. My thoughts turn to our imminent return to normal life. Vacation, alas, is over! Life will settle back into some stressful periods of work balanced with leisure, punctuated with that casual give-and-take of a couple that works together and plays together. We are renewed and ready to get going again...on target and on purpose. This is like having had a summer break, just a bit early!

Before getting back into the swing of real life, we are called to do some genuine introspection. The key questions for both of us to answer, individually, are these: *What am I coping with? Why?*

That's right—what am I coping with? What do I continue to tolerate? What am I putting up with that—if stopped or changed or fixed today—would make things a whole lot better? Consider the second-layer questions below for emergent insights:

- What is most draining me of my available energy?

- Does my work area/environment inspire me? Does it meet my needs?

- Am I tolerating business or personal relationships that drain me?

- Am I investing my time and energy where I should?

- Is there a wicked problem that continues to resurface that I need to resolve?

- Am I working on/involved with/making time for that which matters most? Or am I allowing the busyness of life to swoop me up?

- Are there things I am doing or assumptions I am holding that need to end so that I can move on in a different direction?

- Is there a difficult conversation that's overdue and that has my name on it?

- Am I taking care of myself? My health?

- Am I spending time doing tasks that others should do?

- Am I coping with problematic nuisances that just need to be fixed or replaced (e.g., my temperamental washing machine, a printer that jams)?

What better time than now to move forward with renewed purpose and energy, overcoming those things I've allowed myself to cope with, perhaps for too long.

Join in this introspection! It's probably time that you do this too. Lights On!

Adapted from an e-newsletter article on toleration, by Paige Stapleton and Brian Stark (2011, Authentic Marketing Made Easy*).*

Spring's Promise Fulfilled—or Not?

We left Florida on April 1, driving north and visiting family along the way. We left balmy temperatures and palm trees that seemed to beckon, "Come back, come back!" A couple days later, we were in Charlotte, NC, where spring's promise teased us. The temperature was cool. The beauty surrounding us was glorious—the grass and trees were emerald green and the azaleas were in full bloom. By mid-April we arrived in Niagara, where the dance partners of winter and spring were still in an oscillating struggle over which was to have the lead in their prolonged slow dance. Even the daffodils seemed to be holding back, patiently awaiting nature's signal to safely awaken.

How wonderful to have been afforded multiple observations of spring's unfolding rhythm of change. How intriguing it was to watch winter in Niagara desperately hold on to its last hurrah, adding some snowflakes to this waning winter/spring dance!

So what does this have to do with life or with having our Lights On?

I'm reminded of life's transitions and the model I call the "cauldron of change." When some big change (positive or negative) hits us—when we experience "an ending" that changes our status quo—we enter the cauldron of change. We are destabilized. We may stay in this cauldron for just minutes or for many years—until we are ready to emerge with a "new beginning." This cauldron is the in-between (neutral) transition place where we gain insights, lift ourselves up, and think things through as we shift emotions and energy from an ending to a new beginning. Or we can wallow there; we can have pity parties. Some people resist leaving the cauldron—disengaging, becoming cynical, losing trust, resisting help, and retreating to apathy or despair. They stay in the cauldron until they can find the means to adapt to a new status quo.

As I thought about the prolonged change of seasons in Niagara, I was also reminded that the transition points of our lives (especially those that involve loss) can resemble this oscillating dance—when it is too late to turn back, yet we are not ready to move forward. We are in neutral—not going anywhere; we're between the ending and the new beginning. We may take refuge in our "winters."

Sometimes when there's an "ending" happening in a chapter of our lives, we seem paralyzed. (And that's okay!) Sometimes we're not quite ready to move on, not quite ready to make that "new beginning." Sometimes we need a bit more winter-like slumber, a bit more space, a bit more time to nourish ourselves, a bit more time to prepare—like the tree roots that invest in themselves during the long winter, deepening their time at rest and their sources of nourishment.

A transition (the cauldron place between an ending and a new beginning) might crave the stillness of winter for a bit longer, and that is *endurable* if it *means* something—if it is part of the gradual movement toward a new beginning.

How about you? Have you moved on to spring fulfilled? What is your intuition, your inner teacher, telling you?

Lights On!

Note: This article, written by Claire Knowles, was originally published in Western New York Woman *(www.WNYWoman. com, Spring, 2010).*

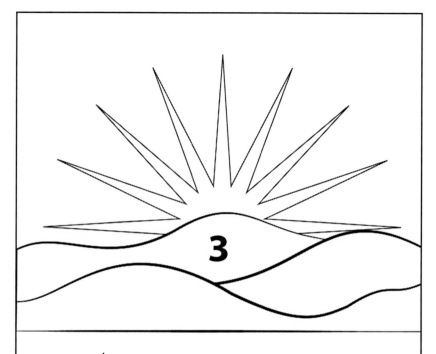

ANCHORING
OUR LIVES

Willow Bends in the Wind

There's a Tai Chi exercise move that's called "willow bends in the wind." It requires that our bodies move like willow trees bent by the force of the wind. Each time we do this posture in class I'm always glad to become *righted* again. It is good to be standing tall and centered, knowing that the force of the imagined wind on my temporary willow-like body is unable to pluck my roots from the ground. Though I'm bent by the gale-force wind, I'm deeply rooted; I'm anchored.

In my consulting work with individuals and with the groups I coach, I look for the basic principles to which they hold firm: the principles on which they live their lives, do their work, and interact/behave with others. I've found that when a person is *not* rooted in principles, then she is easily "blown away by fickle winds." She cannot stand firm. She is like the willow that succumbs to the wind; she has no anchor, no grounding. It is as if she is blowing in the wind.

It is easy to recognize someone who is blowing in the wind and not anchored. Without principles on which to be grounded, you waver; you become rudderless, unsteady in the winds of change. Repetitive patterns of behavior can be lifted up. Without clear, well-set goals, you bounce from one thing to another, lose focus, and lose your sense of direction and coherence with the world. You seldom finish what you start. The tendency is to go negative, blaming everyone and everything. Goal setting, prioritizing, and followthrough get caught up in the swirling whirlwind.

But when a person is really clear on her intentions—-that is, what it is she is trying to do—knows why she is trying to accomplish them, and has committed to the principles by which she needs to live and the ground rules by which she must behave to carry out those intentions—then, she is anchored. She's committed to guiding principles; she's become deeply rooted. She knows how to stay the course even when things are difficult. She knows where her attention must focus.

Here's to you and your "willow bends in the wind" posture. May you personally remain deeply rooted and be very clear about the principles on which you stand. Stand tall! Stand firm! Stay centered and grounded! Always!

Postscript: The answer to the question: "Is it possible to become rooted when most of my life I've been blowing in the wind?" is yes. Process Enneagram© is a mapping process that can assist individuals, groups, and organizations to become principled in their respective endeavors, and to put themselves on the unswerving road to desired achievement.

Some Things Just Seem to Go Together...

S ome things just seem to go together....wine and cheese... shoes and socks...paper and pencil...peanut butter and jelly...love and marriage...cream and sugar...ladies and gentlemen. Each of these pairs represents a dynamic duo. Each is important in relation to the other, and each stays in some degree of balance with the other. Each can stand on its own, yet each is important in its pairing.

Stress, believe it or not, is a lot like this. There is a dynamic balance in play with *eustress*—the good kind of stress, and *distress*—the bad kind of stress. While they are both *stressors*, together they make up *a dynamic stress balance scale*.

Not all news about stress is bad. Pioneer researcher Hans Selye said, "Stress is the spice of life." He termed good stress "eustress." (Eu is a prefix from the Greek meaning "good"). Stress can be a positive force, because eustress represents things that add to the enjoyment and satisfaction of being alive. Intuitively, we are aware of things that bring a sense of eustress and we *crave* them.

The key to stress management is to remind yourself of the importance of balancing eustress and distress. It is therapeutic to find and integrate more eustress to offset the weight of distress— to maintain that dynamic stress balance in our lives.

When you add to the eustress side of your stress balance scale, you'll discover some of your personal passions. Those things that bring you back into balance will be the things that you truly enjoy doing. You'll discover that your eustress is elicited by those activities that bring you joy, ease, and perhaps excitement and a true sense of lightness—the very things that lift you up and make you smile.

The distress side of the balance scale is driven by fear, anger, discontent, unease, and a clear sense of heaviness—all of which are characterized by your complaining. (What do your complaints say about your negative stressors?)

Stress signifies different things for each of us, and both the level of stress and how we handle stress differ from person to person. It is very much like the tension of a balance scale. Too much negative weight tilts us away from being right with the world. *When harmony, coherence, enjoyment, and positive lightness are added, we move back to being centered.* It is important to find the correct amount of eustress to balance out the distress and allow ourselves to be centered most of the time.

So, let's take a closer look at your stress and see how well your distress and eustress stressors are balanced. Draw a balance scale. On one side, list all the negative distressors that are currently weighing you down. Then, list all the positive eustressors that if you add them into your life, are sure to bring you back to center.

Some things just seem to go together!

Note: This article was originally written for and published in Washington Woman Magazine *under the title "Stress Balance," by Claire Knowles, April 2005. This version has been modified.*

Tell Me Your Story

Each one of us has a special story. It has been said that our stories are diminished by the symbolic "hyphen" of the grave marker—the hyphen that denotes the space between a person's birth date and the date of leaving this world. In our heart of hearts we know that our lives stand for something special—something immeasurable and not conveyable by the lowly hyphen. Each of us possesses a vastly important, non-hyphenated story.

In that vein, it is interesting to note (per www.UtneReader.com: "The Focused Life"):

"…that human beings are (supposedly) the only species that actually knows that we must die (at some point). We are also the only ones to know we must find something engaging to focus on in order to pass the time we do have on this earth. As Ralph Waldo Emerson put it, *To fill the hour—that is happiness.*"

We each choose our personal storyline via where, when, and on what we put our attention and focus throughout our lifetime. So, in essence, we've got our lives to contemplate *what we're going to do with our hyphen.*

The point: we each have a story, and within each of our stories there are moments that turn into hours, weeks, months, years, and decades—moments wherein we make pivotal choices and have unique experiences. We learn. We see potential; we dream; we become enthusiastic as we focus and take action. We meet people. We participate in events. We gain new knowledge. We are influenced by and we influence others. We make choices that became the chapter headings for our individual stories. And we can do this consciously—fully aware! We each leave our special mark on the world in some important way—and it is not by way of the hyphen!

If I asked you right now to share your one-minute elevator speech—that crisp capsule of who you are, and what you stand for—and to underscore what matters most to you, what would you share? What is your story? What are you focusing on as your next chapter unfolds?

As you grow and develop, as you fill the hours you're allotted, you move forward through many transitions, many life chapters—similar to the metamorphosis of the butterfly. Sometimes you get stuck in your own cocoon for a bit, sometimes not. Ultimately, you move forward from chapter to chapter to chapter—living out your story. Those numerous chapters—free-standing and combined—tell your beautiful story.

I'd love to hear your story! Lights On!

Postscript: I have only recently had the pleasure of gaining a colleague who is genuinely skilled in Life Purpose coaching. Add this to the mix: Wouldn't it be wonderful if every person knew their Life Purpose theme and their true mission in life? Imagine the joy of doing what you were meant to do!

The Tag-Along Gurney and Second Chances

There's a haunting TV ad for a pharmaceutical drug that is intended to prevent repeat heart attack occurrence. In this ad an empty gurney follows closely behind a person, wherever that person goes. The gurney, of course, invokes an image that there might not be a second chance, while the words of the ad underscore the value of the drug for attaining a second chance at life.

I've had heart concerns, so I can relate to this ad. I expect that most people, as they age, and regardless of their health situations, can also relate to the value of second chances, more opportunities to get it right—not just in health, but in the fullness of our lives.

Part of my work is in teaching—specifically about living systems and resultant patterns that show up, both in organizations and throughout our individual lives. Living systems are about patterns. As living systems, we consciously learn and reflect on our experiences. We can visualize possibilities for the future and then prepare for them.

We learn, we grow, we change, we adapt, we co-create, and we seek coherence with and meaning from our environment and relationships with others. We are constantly in motion, with a built-in guidance system to continue to grow and develop, to move forward.

So we are geared to evolving, to metamorphosis, to change, to having second, third, fourth, and numerous chances to seize new opportunities, new learning, new growth. We are ever-renewing (even at the cellular level) all the time—so this particular image of the gurney, one of impending death—is extremely haunting to us. It represents the opposing force to life and to renewing ourselves.

I like the idea of being human and of having second chances (and more) in all phases of our lives.

We get chances for redos.

We get chances for relearning.

We get chances to forgive and to be forgiven.

We get chances to move forward.

We just have to say yes when that choice shows up for us. The action steps are ours to take. Life is ours to embrace. Lights On!

Pluck a Star from the Sky

About 40 minutes into our Tai Chi exercise class, and with focused concentration, we perform this pose, "pluck a star from the sky." It requires that, while alternating arms and hands, you stretch upward as high as you can, while simultaneously lifting your heels off the ground. As the star is plucked, your feet return fully to the ground, centered again, and the hand and arm return to your side. Next, the alternate arm and hand rise up, heels off the floor again—yes, to pluck another star from the sky, one at a time. This stretch feels wonderful. Re-anchoring to the ground feels wonderful. The pose includes breathing in deeply as the arm and hand rise, and fully exhaling as the arm and hand return to your side. The stars—all ripe for plucking— are abundant and imaginary, limited only by one's energy to continue reaching for them.

I can't help but think about plucking stars from the sky. Which ones would I choose? There must be special ones containing the breadth of my wish list. After all, I can still remember the nursery rhyme about wishing upon a special star. We've all had that experience!

> *Star light, star bright,*
> *First star I've seen tonight,*
> *I wish I may, I wish I might,*
> *Have the wish I wish tonight.*

As a mature, consciously-aware adult, this extension pose is never complete until I ask myself, what is it that I wish for today? Which of these stars—waiting for me and requiring me to stretch upward to reach—is mine to pluck next? What is it that is mine to dream? Mine to desire? What requires me to stretch even more? What am I trying to accomplish? What new work or what new joy is awaiting my grasp? With what divine energy should I be connecting? What is it that I am to do next as a catalyst for growth? What further stretching action am I beckoned to deliver?

Each time I stretch upward like this, I sense the true act of reaching, of striving, of extending myself. As my heels leave the floor, I'm igniting that catalyst in me to stretch just a bit more, to reach up just a bit further. First, I feel the stretch. Next is the realization that there is now more action for me to do as I become reconnected with the world again, heels down, fully grounded, re-anchored, remotivated. "Plucking a star from the sky" is more than a physical Tai Chi pose; this has a deeper, metaphorical meaning. Like a parable, it speaks to the student on several levels.

For me, simply performing this pose while breathing deeply provides me with my celestial twinkling. I've got a lot of *star plucking* to do yet. I have much more to reach for as I grow forward. There is much more work for me to do when I'm grounded and centered. There is more joy within my reach. How about for you? What's on your star-plucking list?

Postscript: A few years ago, there was a lot of press about a Star Registry. By sending in a certain amount of money, you could actually claim a star; that is, register your or your loved one's name. That star was then renamed in this registry for the person desiring a celestial connection. While I found that most interesting, I'd rather contemplate the Universe as so abundant in its offerings, with stars too numerous to count, fully knowing that our dreams, desires, goals, and, yes, a celestial connection are all there for us already—free!—we just have to reach out, stretch, grasp, and then take the actions required of us. Lights On!

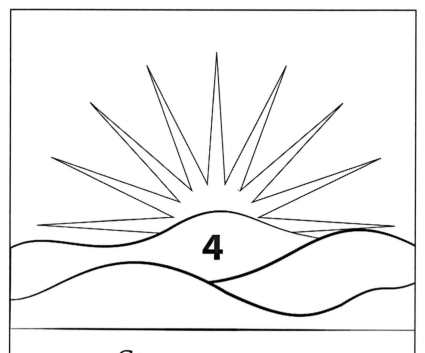

STARTING
ANEW

Reflections

Look in the mirror. What do you see? Look deeper. What are you *becoming*?

Look beyond what is there. Do you see the possibilities? Do you have the courage to consciously *become*? What is the silent signal that beckons you forth? I'm reminded of the giant oak tree that is beckoned forth from the acorn seed. Your life is beckoned forth too. You are naturally drawn, by your human nature, to continue to grow and develop, to move forward. There may be resistance along that path. Sometimes you may stray. Sometimes you may sleepwalk through parts of the journey. Sometimes you may hide from yourself. Sometimes you may stay stuck in your own cocoon—trying to convince yourself *not* to move forward. Sometimes we stagnate.

Does this sound familiar? "The way of cowardice is to embed ourselves in a cocoon, in which we perpetuate our habitual patterns. When we are constantly recreating our basic patterns of behavior and thought, we never have to leap into fresh air or onto fresh ground. We stagnate." (Chogyman Trungpa, *Shambhala: The Sacred Path of the Warrior*)

Perhaps we allow ourselves to stay in our cocoons, or to go through life sleepwalking *by abdicating the personal responsibility that's required to grow, to become.* The caterpillar cannot be both a caterpillar and a butterfly—while metamorphosis may be frightening, we know that as we reflect deep within ourselves, we find the strength to walk that next part of our path. Here's to rebuilding and strengthening ourselves from the inside out—to *becoming*—just like the butterfly!

We learn from self-help literature that it supposedly takes a minimum of 25 days for the brain to build the neural links required to make a new behavior a habit. The trouble with cocoon-type habits is that they preserve the status quo, making dramatic improvement unlikely. If we want more out of life, we must be willing to evaluate and replace some of those habits and rituals with more constructive ones. Here are some examples: turning off the TV and, instead, going for a brisk walk or doing something positive from that list of to-dos. Here's to displacing those old habits and rituals that no longer serve one's growth and development!

Affirmation: Today I boldly make my commitment to learning and growing, to shedding old habits that stifle me. I affirm my own metamorphosis—releasing the past and moving into my beauty and greatness—and I know that is stronger than my commitment to staying the same! Lights On!

Sometimes We All Need a Little Push!

There's an inspirational and heart-touching video from Simple Truths about the mother eagle having to push her fledgling eaglets from a nest that is situated on the highest pinnacle. It is the hardest thing she has to do, because the eaglets have never flown and there's only one chance to get it right. It's a test of courage and a tribute to her inner knowing that in order to be an eagle and fulfill the eagle destiny, her eaglets have to fly—then, and only then, will they soar! She has to trust that there will be sufficient wind beneath their wings!

Sometimes each of us needs a push too. A push to set personal and professional goals. A push to follow through. A push to move forward with a leap of faith. A push to do what we know we need to do. A push to get on with it! A push to start again. A push to move something through to completion.

There's an old story of two coaching gurus, made famous by Joe Vitale in *The Key*. One guru is experienced, the other, a novice. The novice asks the elder, "Why is it that when I coach someone and they say they are going to do this or that, that several weeks later I find that they haven't even started to do this or that? Instead, they've just muttered the words of wishful thinking and there's been no real action?" The wise guru shared "That is because they just aren't hungry enough." The novice then asks, "Well, how can someone become hungry enough to do what they say they really want to do?" The elder guru then shared, "Something else is feeding them....and you have to find out what that is....because until they are ready to stop feeding on what is keeping them in their current state, they'll not be hungry enough to act; their words of intention and their actions will remain in conflict."

The moral of the story: perhaps you need a push to get you started toward your goals. Get really clear on what it is you want to have happen, to do, or to be. Then find out what is keeping you stuck right now. What's feeding your present comfort zone? What's kept you from moving forward before? Whatever has been keeping you from moving forward needs to be worked on at the same time as determining what you must do to move forward. There are chains to break and there are new things to do!

Then, start anew!

Be the person you are meant to be—fulfill your destiny. Just as the eaglet has to learn to fly before she can soar, so you can succeed at the change you're focusing upon…with just a little push from your inner personal courage. Go! Don't be afraid of falling…there's wind beneath your wings!

---

*"We have all walked the high wire of circumstance at times. We recognize the gravity pull of the earth, yet we choose **not** to fall." ~Martha Graham (dancer and choreographer)*

Time Is Our Gift

Tick…tick…tick…tick…

How does the passage of time influence our lives? How does our inner need to grow and develop, to move forward, to turn over new leaves (again and again), fit with the passage of time?

Think of a new beginning…like the beginning of a new fern unfurling. Think about our cells ever-renewing. Think about turning the calendar page to a new day, a new year, a new decade, the dimension of time factored into our lives as we embrace new beginnings. Times Square in New York City is aptly named for the modern-day year-ending and year-beginning celebrations— it is famous for the time countdown and the ball drop. At that one precise moment, we turn over the new leaf, the new calendar page. We start anew. We begin again.

There is an ancient connection to an archetypal image too—the connection to Janus, the Roman god, who stands at the precise place of end of life and new life. Janus, depicted as Father Time, stands and looks back reflectively at what was; at the very same moment, he also looks forward to the newness that is about to emerge, depicted as a new baby, filled with promise.

Janus is considered the keeper of that transition threshold—the tiny sliver of space that marks the boundary between the past and the future, between what was and what can be. It is a transition place, a momentary pass-through, bursting with possibility. This is a transition place we have all experienced in our letting go of the old and in our embracing of the new. We know this transcendent place well. Indeed, our lives are continually marked by transition and growth.

The lunar cycles are a reminder of our connection to the deep natural patterns of renewal. In our daily connections to these deeper patterns, we note the ticking away of time as we experience sunrise and sunset—the beginning promise of the day, ending with the fullness of this very same day. Indeed, our lives are marked with the patterns of time as it ticks ever-forward. Spring, summer, fall, and winter. A season to plant, a season to grow, a season to harvest, a season to lie fallow.

We have many opportunities to look back and assess the various aspects of our lives, but is it not of greater importance to *keep reflecting on how we use our gift of time* as the months, the seasons, the days, and the years tick by? We cannot stop the clock from ticking away the time. But we can be the best we can be within the time we are allotted.

We progress quickly through the various quarters of the year— each filled with promise, each presenting changing seasons, all patterns we know deeply. Each day presents us with a new opportunity to become what we choose to become. Is it not worth reflecting that each month has a new moon? That each day has a new sunrise? A new beginning? That each dimension provides us insight into deeper patterns of renewal and letting go? We have, on a yearly, monthly, daily, yes, even hourly basis, the capacity to comprehend the world, our lives, our goals, our endeavors, our inspirations, and to cultivate our work, our gifts, our talents, our skills, and our contributions to that gift of time. The clock ticks…

So, as the months and days pass by—ask yourself:

- What am I doing with this great gift of *time*?

- In what ways am I becoming even better?

- In what ways am I reflecting and renewing?

- What new leaves should I be turning over?

- Am I sunsetting old, worn-out ideas and emerging with new potential?

- Am I developing my gifts and continuing to learn and to deepen my presence?

- Am I fulfilling those personal and professional promises I've made?

- To what am I newly committed?

Here's to making the changes you envision as necessary in your life in *each month* and *each day* going forward. With each new moon and full moon, with each sunrise and sunset, may you sense those deeper patterns that spark renewal and that compel you to make the best use of your gift of time.

Tick…tick…tick…tick…

"The spot of grace: What's unfinished for you to give? In the thousands of moments that we string together to make up our lives, there are some where time seems to change its shape and a certain light falls across our ordinary path. We stop searching for purpose…we become it. Looking back we might describe these moments as times when we were at our best, when the gifts we were born with and the talents we have developed were braided with what we love and with the needs of the world." ~Dawna Markova

---

New Chapters: Taking Stock and Moving Ahead!

"If you continue to do what you've always done, you will continue to have what you've always had. If you want different, and if you do different, you will have different."
~Anthony Robbins

My colleague, Peter Wendel, sent me his article called "Stop, Start, Continue," which detailed an interesting activity for a business group, organization, or a team to explore, particularly at times when *new beginnings* are needed. It noted that, too often, groups just keep going along, doing what they have been doing—which, over time, puts them more and more out of synch with their environment. The approach provided a way to stop, take stock of the team's current situation, refocus, and make decisions on how to move forward. I thought it was excellent!

As I contemplated this, I noted that it is an appropriate time for individuals to pause for reflection, and that a similar approach was important for the *renewing person* too. We've all participated in resolutions made at the turn of the New Year. We tend to *put out the old* and *bring in the new*. We tend to get rid of the clutter, re-energize, and focus. The remaining question is... *"Are we putting our energy into what really matters?"*

Completions – Look back over the last 6 to 18 months and list your personal accomplishments. What had you hoped to accomplish? What did you actually accomplish? List what you've done and include in that list the things that you stopped doing—often because they were no longer valid, or because other things interfered. This list should include the accomplishments in your home and family life, work life, relationship-building, and in your social, personal, and spiritual development too. Be as specific as you can be. Let yourself bask a bit as you celebrate your achievements! Take note of which heading is getting the most of your energy and attention. Did these goals support your personal mission? Did you move forward?

Continuations – Look at what you are currently doing. What are you engaged in? What are those things that are *still in process*, and *still in progress*? What needs more time, more nurturing? More contemplation? Can you identify the next milestones? Can you identify which have priority?

Beginnings – Stephen Covey, in *The 7 Habits of Highly Effective People*, notes that one of the habits is to "begin with the end in mind." What are your hopes, dreams, and new high-priority goals? Can you see the end results? Do they support your personal mission? Covey notes that: "All things are created twice." It is based on the premise that there is a mental or first creation, followed by a physical or second creation. Covey writes: "How different our lives are when we really know what is *deeply important* to us, and, keeping that picture in mind, we manage ourselves each day to be and to do what really matters most."

I love that phrase, "what matters most." Do you know what *matters most* to you? *Deliberately* review your goals, plans, hopes, dreams, and desires for each of the headings above. Can you identify what the end result looks like? Can you visualize that for each of your goals? Can you visualize some milestone markers to note along the journey to the end results? Have you asked whether these are all achievable? Are your expectations reasonable? What do you need? Do you need support? How will you seek that support?

Next, ask yourself:

- What is so important about achieving this particular goal?

- Is there a principle at stake?

- Does one hinge on another?

- Look at which of your life achievement headings is getting most of the energy you have to give. Is there some re-allotment necessary?

- Somewhere amid the concerns of wanting to do everything, to achieve what is possible, and to be available to others, is also the need to take care of yourself. Have you made that a priority? How do you sustain yourself? And lastly, where is your joy?

There are a lot of questions to contemplate in this article. Perhaps you might even think that it sounds a bit preachy. The questions, however, are offered, not as provocative questions in a sermon, but rather in the spirit of *advocacy for you*. The questions are for you to grab hold of—if you want to—to ensure that you are moving forward along a path that unfolds consistently with *what matters most* for you.

"In the absence of clearly-defined goals, we become strangely loyal to performing daily acts of trivia until ultimately we are enslaved by it." ~Robert Heinlein

---

About Making Positive Personal Change

Perhaps your goal-setting and follow-through needs a bit of a boost. Or perhaps you are struggling with what is needed to make a lasting change in your life. Even if you've failed before—that's okay! Focus on how you can determine your best chance to succeed going forward. Where should you place your energy and efforts? What would derail you?

Intentional positive change is most likely to occur when certain factors are present. Why not examine your personal situation with respect to these factors? Be mindful of these:

- **Have you clearly defined the goal?** the target? the mile-markers? Are you clear on what success will look like when the goal is achieved? Do you know why you want to achieve this?

- **Do you believe that you can accomplish this?** Do you believe that you will reach this goal/target? You absolutely have to be convinced in your heart of hearts that you will achieve it. (Often goals fall by the wayside because the strength of this belief is too weak.)

- **Are you clear on what the positive motivating force is for you to accomplish this goal?** What is the positive reward for you? What is the good that will come out of this when you reach your goal/target? Can you clearly embrace having this positive reward happen for you? Do you genuinely long for it?

- **Are you clear on what the negative motivating force is for NOT accomplishing this goal?** What is the pain or the discomfort that will occur? What is the negative reinforcement—what will happen to you that you don't want to have happen? How strong is your desire for not wanting the negative consequence to happen? Have you a deep sense of rejecting this negative?

- **Have you thoroughly thought through and identified what the means are?** And do you know how to acquire the means to reach the target from where you are right now? Do the plans make sense? Does the timeframe make sense? What are these means? New technology? New skills? A change in habits? Willpower boost? Exercise? Schedule changes? Prioritization calendar?

- **Have you thought about what precisely is anchoring you to "the old way"?** What needs to be put in place to undo the very things that have been keeping you in the status quo? What do you need to do differently to break those chains? What system changes are necessary? What new agreements?

- **Are you prepared and committed to learn what you need to learn to acquire these means?** Are you ready to fully integrate this change into your life? Have you voiced this decision that this goal is your personal intent? Does the universe know...so it can help to attract it into your life?

Go for it!

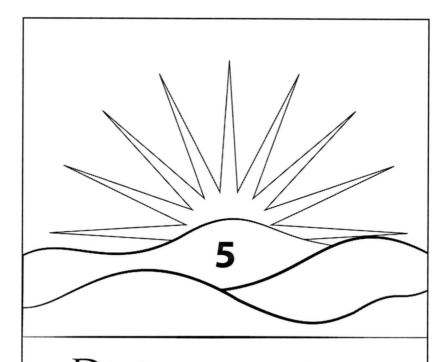

5

DECLUTTERING
OUR LIVES

Simplicity...on the Inside

We know when our lives are in a frantic blur. We know when we are craving simplicity. We know when we need to become calm and to breathe! So the dilemma isn't about knowing what we need, *it is about loving ourselves enough to do it.*

There have been many things written about simplifying our lives. Perhaps that is because life has become too frantic and we need to find that inner oasis, a space where we can renew, a place where we can be nurtured, a welcoming space where we can practice self-love. We live in a fast-paced world, often barraged with information overload. Many of us who know this too-much-to-do/no-time-to-breathe place have concluded that it is time to simplify our lives—beginning with our inner lives. Have you heard yourself echo these words?

- *Spend time outdoors*. Seek the restorative and inspirational power of nature. Take in some sunshine. Breathe…breathe… breathe (fresh air). And bring some nature inside—herb gardens, fresh cut flowers, and plants are a great way to bring refreshing life into your home environment.

- *Get rid of clutter* around you: in your home and work environment. The less clutter, the more energy you will have! When there is clutter around us, we feel closed in. Declutter—make space. Organize. Ridding yourself of what you no longer need creates an incredible sense of freedom.

- *Get rid of the external noise and internal mind chatter* that prevents you from hearing your inner voice. Find your stillness. Leave the iPod at home; drive without playing the radio. Carve out some quiet space. Get in touch again with your inner teacher. Listen! When life is moving so fast

77

and you are running at a frantic pace, you cannot hear your intuitive teacher.

- *Slow down some of your daily routines*. Eat slowly—without distractions. Pace yourself! Instead of multitasking, try seeing some project through to completion. Relax. Put on some soft, slow-beat music; change the rhythm. What rhythm resonates best for you?

- *Eliminate the things you don't want in your life*...those negative nasty habits like engaging in gossip and idle chatter, fuming over past events, or worrying about the future. Rise above the office bickering; instead, find something really good to focus on. Disentangle.

- *Read books and listen to CDs* that provide inspiration, lift you up, and move you forward. Set your intention to grow and develop in new ways. Be deliberate. Broaden your world. Take a class. Visit a museum. Go to a concert.

- *Find ways to introvert*, to go into yourself and do what brings you some inner joy and peace. Sit quietly. Go within. Listen to your inner voice. Take time for you. Meditate.

- *Face your inner fears.* Work past what is holding you back. We all sense the negative and contract inward, pulling back at times. Do you know when that happens? Make that list of all the things you want to do...*but* (the things you have been resisting). Determine what is behind the *buts.* Conversely, congratulate yourself too. Yes...excuse me while I cheer...I just did the thing I fear! Enjoy those moments when you exude confidence. Build on them.

- *Make it a habit to develop gratitude.* Keep a gratitude journal—record daily. When we are in a grateful state of mind, we attend to our well-being. Think about just three things daily for which you are grateful! Gratitude provides a positive lift.

- *Use affirmations and declare yourself.* How do you want your life to be? What are you are going to do to affirm your goals (to have, to do, and to be). What matters most?

- *Ask for help when you need it!* So many women take on more than anyone would expect of them. Asking for help is one of the best ways to carve out some time for yourself. Ask! Expect help from others.

- *Trust!* Accept living with ambiguity and not requiring certainty in your life. Enjoy each day, one at a time. Expect surprises!

- *Celebrate and savor your successes.* Encourage the next. Applaud yourself. Smile!

- *Breathe.* And breathe again. Deeper.

In my workshops I will often use a Hoberman's sphere to demonstrate both the frantic pace of our lives and the contrasting calm needed in our lives. When we say we need to take the time to *breathe,* there's no better illustration. Deep breathing is calming. (My audience makes that "Ahhhhhh" sound every time!) Hoberman's spheres are available in most toy stores and essentially are a plastic geometric-patterned ball-like object that expands and contracts, indicative of both the frenzy and the calmness of our lives.

Adapted from Finding Inner Simplicity, *by Elaine St. James, 2002.*

"When we find ourselves devoid of passion and purpose, the first thing we need to do is STOP. But that's not easy. The rest of the world is zooming by at full speed. Left alone with ourselves, we can become nervous and self-critical about what we should or should not be doing and feeling. This can be so uncomfortable that we look for any distraction rather than allowing ourselves the space to be as we are. It is in our stillness and our listening that we hear; that we know."

~Dawna Markova

January Sweep

It seems like each year, early in the month of January, there is a special day designated as "National Clean Off Your Desk Day"! It is intended to coincide with returning to work after the holiday season and making a fresh start. You've probably heard the phrase "Less Clutter...More Energy!" That makes great sense.

What about your internal personal clutter? Have you let go of what's old and no longer useful? It is difficult to create anything new until you do! Think about that! When the cobwebs of the past are sticking around, they hinder us from moving forward.

Having a designated *sweep day* does make good sense. It seems wise to me to have a strategy to start off the first month of the year, or more often, without having internal personal cobwebs hanging around, and with a clean desk. This helps us move forward, to work toward new goals.

There is something good about *being right with ourselves*. It is refreshing to have a clean slate, to start again, to be in synch with our inner need to move forward. Yet to move forward, we have to let go of the negative cluttering—the residue—whether it be on our desks, in our lives, or within our environment.

In the home that my husband and I lived in for over 20 years, there was a beautiful wood-burning fireplace. We decided, for fire-prevention reasons, to hire a chimney sweep to clean out the built-up soot. On the appointed day, the chimney sweep arrived, dressed like the chimney sweeps made famous in *Mary Poppins*. While the advertisement in the phone book showed the picture of the chimney sweep in full tuxedo tails, I was surprised to see him dressed that way. I loved this man's attitude, his charm, and his supreme pride in his work and profession. He was not just cleaning our fireplace and flue, he was continuing a centuries-old tradition. He had a sense of purpose about him, and a destiny to fulfill. He whistled as he worked. He twirled his brooms. He purposely smudged his nose. It was a noteworthy performance. Professionally, at the onset, he shared that by the time he finished his chimney sweeping work that day, he would have created the best fireplace free-flow of upward air conveyance that there could be! There would be no residue.

There would be nothing left over to interfere with the ambience of our fireplace going forward. He, with his talent, skills, and presence, *was performing a January sweep*—gone would be the old residue. He was making way for the future—providing the space and free-flowing air draft so that the real beauty of the embers could be safely enjoyed well into the future.

Now, that's a January sweep!

Spring Cleaning Includes Removing the Cobwebs That Stifle One's Spirit Too

It is spring. We've had that first really sunny day. The one that boosts you up and moves you forward. The one that provides the impetus to clean the garage, to thoroughly clean the car (inside and out), and even to clean one's closets. Yes, it is time to sort through one's closets again, put away winter, reorganize, and ready one's wardrobe for spring.

Have you thought about cleaning out your internal closet cobwebs so that your spirit (both personal and professional) is primed for renewal too? Have you examined your self-esteem? Our psyche benefits when we are lifted up! Possessing a mindset of positivity is a choice. Let's shake out those mind-closet negatives and move forward into spring with positive gusto!

Psychologists have a lot to say about raising self-esteem and about discovering ways to lift up the positives—all for an improved sense of well-being. You can refocus negative thoughts if you choose. You can have only one thought in your head at a time. It can bring you up, or it can drag you down. You choose. The same holds true with engaging in gratitude journaling. As you write about that for which you are grateful, the negative is not present. Can you hold that positive space?

We have the freedom of choice—that is, we choose our response to whatever happens to us in life. So we can surround ourselves with ego boosters, instead of ego busters. We can do things that make us feel competent and give us a feeling of accomplishment. We can develop thick skin and deflect the barbs from those "invalidators" who try to bring us down. As Miguel Ruiz writes in his book, *The Four Agreements,* "Don't take anything personally." Those negatives simply reflect whatever is going on with those who deliver the barbs. You can get hugs and give hugs, because physical contact generates an internal response (consciously or unconsciously) that builds positive self-awareness, as you perceive someone cares about you, and vice versa!

Here's an easy jump-start strategy for your spirit's renewal— being consciously aware of your own positive words and phrases: I can; I will; I am; I love; I create; I do; and yes, I accept the challenge! Concurrently, let's remove the negative words and phrases like: I can't; I won't; well, maybe; I don't know; I don't care; and no, that's a problem.

After all, there's nothing worse when cleaning closets than indecision around what stays, what goes, and what comes in anew. When it comes to our internal workings, we want a whole walk-in closet full of positive, revitalizing energy! Lights On!

"Everything and everyone either moves you closer to where you want to be (on your development path) or farther away from where you want to be. Nothing is neutral." ~Larry Winget

---

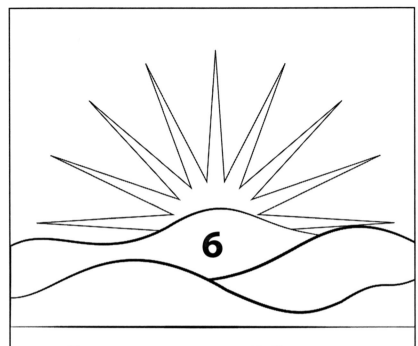

6

SHINING YOUR LIGHT!

On Being the Best You Can Be!

The old Sunday School song about not letting your light stay hidden under a bushel basket, but rather to "let it shine, let it shine, let it shine" was reinforced for me this week.

I was handling a stack of angel cards. The one that fell out of the deck seemed to speak to me; "light" was the word on the card. Immediately I thought about what author Debbie Ford calls the "eternal flame" or "eternal light" that resides within each person. We each have this inner light essence—it is the keeper of our life force. When this light glows, we feel strong, centered, confident, and up. When the flame's light is low, we are vulnerable, frail, weak, and down.

The size and the brightness of our light essence affects those around us. Our light can impact others. At times, our own light goes out and we are renewed by the spark of another! Think about what happens when you are around positive, uplifting people. Think about what happens when you are continually subjected to criticism.

There are choices that we each make and behaviors that we each engage in, that drain that light and essence from us. Conversely, there are choices we make that can actually fuel our flame, provide sustenance, and help us glow brightly. I prefer the latter!

I clearly connect with the word *light*. My name, Claire, comes from the French, meaning *bright* and *illustrious*. I love seeing and being in the light—the sunrise, the sunset, the light shining through the woods. Yes, *light* seems to be a word attached to my life, a potent concept for my soul. I've been writing my Lights On! articles for the specific purpose of illuminating—of being a catalyst for growth in my own little way.

A colleague has been encouraging me to keep writing; there is so much more to share in a world that is hungry for our collective gifts: yours, hers, mine. Yes, each one of us is traveling our own path—trying to discover our own personal light essence and trying to find those specific gifts to bring forth into this world— because that light within us is aglow!

Postscript:

> *This little light of mine....I'm gonna let it shine!*
> *Hide it under a bushel?*
> *No! I'm gonna let it shine,*
> *let it shine, let it shine, let it shine!*

Recommended reading: The Right Questions: Ten Essential Questions to Guide You to an Extraordinary Life *by Debbie Ford.*

Co-creating Your Life with a High-Beam Focus

When interviewed prior to a women's professional event, I was asked about the questions raised by women whom I have coached. Are there recurrent themes? The answer is *yes*. Here are some of them:

Emptiness:

Is that all there is? Life has to be more than what I'm experiencing. I seem to be devoid of passion about anything.

Life struggles:

Life is just too busy, too harried to take the time to stop, think, reflect, or change. How do I break out of this whirlwind? How do I make sense of things? Why does life have to be so hard? Everything seems to be a struggle. It seems like I take two steps forward, and then step backward into a hole again.

The life transition / the subtle nudge to move forward:

Something is nudging me to change, to move forward, to transition. Yet I have no idea as to what, when, why, or where. I feel so disconnected—like I don't belong to or identify with this work or place anymore. How do I know whether this is the right path I should be taking? What else should I be doing?

Becoming the best I can be:

I'm successful; I love what I do, but I know I can do more, be more, become even more fulfilled. How can I be the best leader I can be?

Successfully combining family and career can be difficult. How do successful professional women combine family and career so that there is coherence, balance, and achievement?

Teams/organizations:

Everything is always chaotic. Everyone is out for themselves. By the end of the day I just want to scream! We just seem to spin our wheels. We keep recycling things over and over again. The goal posts keep moving.

Negative, self-defeating talk:

Our words are predictive. One of the recurrent themes for some women is in holding a negative view of themselves and their world. Paying attention to the actual words that are coming from one's own mouth is important and telling. What are you complaining about? Bemoaning? Belittling? Are your own words inviting more chaos and disharmony?

Lights On! Guidance:

As a personal, life, executive, and organizational/team coach, I enjoy helping people create the space for choosing personal growth and development, for turning on one's inner light, and for getting very clear on intentions and followthrough, principles, and behaviors. I particularly enjoy working with teams and organizations to get very focused and to become most effective in the work they are chartered to accomplish.

Using the metaphor of "Lights On!":

If you are journeying through life with your personal light dimmed by negativity...

If you are unable to envision (shine a light on) the future you want because you are too harried to stop and reflect...

If you know you are being nudged into a life transition, yet it seems so unclear...then it is time to consciously shift to using your high-beam headlights...all the time!

Most successful professional women, including those who combine family and career:

- Hold clear intentions and take time to renew them daily.

- Envision their futures.

- Are principle-based leaders.

- Prepare for, and are open to, their futures unfolding.

- Are able to discern what is important and what is not, so that what they attend to connects to their higher expectations.

- Are organized, but do not micromanage.

- Trust. They can live with ambiguity.

- Remain open to being surprised, keeping their eyes open and maintaining high awareness.

When you shift your thinking to higher intention, you attract that into your life. It is a conscious choice. You can shift today!

All of the above statements reflect the individual *becoming aware*.

Noticing is the first step! Some are consciously wanting to break out of what I call *chrysalis paralysis*. For some, there is a recognition that life isn't unfolding well and that something has to change, but they feel stuck—*almost paralyzed.* Others know that things are in disharmony and chaotic, yet refuse to stop and examine why or how to break the patterns, the self- imposed prisons, that are limiting their lives. For others, there is a clear sense of knowing; there is a stimulus to be open to a new change, to gather strength, to find one's voice and move forward, albeit perplexed by the ambiguity of it all. While some are stuck inside their chrysalis, others responsibly and trustingly move forward and emerge as the butterfly.

We are always transitioning; we are always in change. Life is always presenting change to us! We are *in metamorphosis*. We are likened to the caterpillar. The caterpillar attaches itself to a protected place while it undergoes a transformation into a chrysalis. The butterfly that emerges has a whole new life in a very different, exciting form. We, too, are in a constant process of change. We need to be clear on our intentions, and then we must attend to them with aligned actions. It requires *high-beam focus*. Lights On!

All That Sparkles Is You!

I spent a good part of this past winter in St. Pete Beach, Florida. Every so often, when the sun is positioned just right, and the Gulf water's ripples are formed in a certain rhythm, one can see *sparkling water*. It is like seeing a host of sparkles dancing on the water. It is a wondrous phenomenon. Yet, if you look in the opposite direction—where the sun's angled rays differ—there is *no* sparkling water. No sparkles.

Instead, you'll see beautiful blue water with rippling waves, but no sparkles.

As I reflect on our lives, we have that special sparkle at times too—knowing what we stand for, knowing what evokes our passion, and knowing what brings us joy. All are important to grasp and manifest into our lives. What is it in you that sparkles for others to see?

Even if we're not currently sparkling, we are still beautiful— like experiencing that sunny day at the water's edge from the different viewpoint. More and more frequently our lives can sparkle like the *sparkling water*—when we live our lives with purpose, with meaning, and with passion. We sparkle when we allow ourselves to be "up." Then we glisten for all to see.

It was Henry David Thoreau who said "Most men lead lives of quiet desperation, and go to their graves with their song still in them." Those are lives that are devoid of *sparkle*. Isn't it great that each of us does have a measure of that inner, positive sparkle—even if it needs to be coaxed forward sometimes?

Sometimes life gets out of balance; we're overstressed and we lose that sparkling *me essence*. You can help your inner sparkle— that inner light that wants to shine—to emerge if you want it to!

Each of us has an emotional ladder on which we move up and down (consciously or unconsciously). It is our barometer for sparkle! On the top of the ladder are the high emotions like Joy, Love, Appreciation, Passion, Enthusiasm, Happiness, Optimism, Hopefulness, and Contentment. At the bottom of the ladder are negative emotions like Fear, Grief, Despair, Powerlessness, Insecurity, Jealousy, Hatred, Revenge, Anger, Discouragement, and Blame. And in the middle of the ladder are the emotions of Boredom, Pessimism, Frustration, Overwhelm, Disappointment, Doubt, and Worry.

Whenever we've lost our sparkle, we're probably hovering in the lower emotions and the task is to consciously move up the emotional scale. Find something to be grateful about, even in the midst of the difficulty. Find a positive spin to put on even the worst of circumstances. Move back up the emotional ladder. Deliberately make yourself move into a higher emotion. Find that sparkle again. Glisten for all to see!

"What aileth thee? We all have islands of fear inside us, but we also all have continents of wisdom and trust. How do we find our way to them when we are not educated in the interior dimension? These inner landscapes hold the patterns of our passion and purpose. Without knowing how to journey there, our lives remain unlived." ~Dawna Markova

---

Postscript: Thus, we have to learn to access the center core of our being. We have to know where we are and deliberately choose to move up our emotional ladder!

Recommended reading: The Amazing Power of Deliberate Intent *by Esther and Jerry Hicks and* I Will Not Die an Unlived Life *by Dawna Markova.*

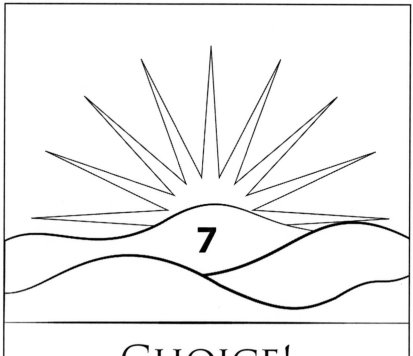

7

CHOICE!

As Shakespeare Says: To Be or Not to Be...
It's Your Choice!

The calendar page turned over to the month of June, and with that transition came another birthday. For me it is another special life-date, and the celebration of another year. I'm reminded of Sophie Tucker's old adage about the secret to a long life: keep breathing!

I'm a Gemini. Perhaps that's the reason that I'm so keen to notice the dualities of this life: hot/cold, positive/negative, strong/gentle, courage/cowardice, kind/mean, forward/back, yes/no, sickness/health. I don't notice these dualities fleetingly, but rather, hold them as the basic construct of the hugely dynamic world around us. Dualities are everywhere; our world is one of constant choice. We each make choices in every moment of every day...we each choose where, what, and how we will be.

My view is that there is a wide range of choice within each of these dualities—all the time. It is like a sliding scale. Imagine that you are a stick—a stick containing all the dualities of life and a stick on which you move up and down the scale all the time, depending on where and how you choose to be in any given moment. And, as life moves on, you tend to find various *set points* along the way that seem to work for you. You might be very comfortable in an optimist setting (as opposed to pessimist); or you might be shy (as opposed to bold). While the set points become grooves because of repeated choices, we each still have free choice to move anyplace along the scale, at any time. Our choices, of course, reflect our growing knowledge base, beliefs, values, life experiences, maturity, and personal and professional development.

My coaching brings me in touch with many women in the workplace who are hugely frustrated with behaviors they bump up against on a daily basis. The teaching of the dualities of life is this: everyone has their own stick—their own choice of where they will be at any given moment. And while you may influence where that other person moves on their stick, you cannot control that other person's choice. So if another person is mean-spirited (as opposed to kind), or deceptive (as opposed to straightforward), or continually puts someone down (as opposed to lifting them up), they are choosing their point on that duality scale at that moment in time. You may try to persuade that person to think or act differently, but in the end, it still is their choice. It is about them, not about you.

And the lesson is: *the only thing you can do is to choose your own response*. Will you remain a class act? Fully professional? Or will you drop down in the mud? Will you stand up, or whither? Will you be courageous or cowardly or somewhere in between? Will you be kind or snarly? Will you back-bite or be conciliatory? Will you move on or begrudge? Will you help or hinder? Will you be positive or negative? What will your response be on the sliding scale of how you choose to be? It is solely *your* choice. Life is renewing and the dualities of choice are there for us every day. (And yes, every new birthday gives me another chance to improve my set points!)

The Serenity Prayer really does fit here: "God, grant me the serenity to accept the things I cannot change, the courage to change the things I can, and the wisdom to know the difference."

But I must add this: *Accepting things one cannot change does <u>not</u> mean "condoning" those things. It means accepting that some things are not yours to change, and are not your battle to fight; they are not yours to control, nor should you put any energy into* *them.* Rather, put your focus, energy, and attention elsewhere—on the important things where you can make a difference—with your own stick.

We do our best to make the world better in every moment by choosing our responses wisely—by being shining examples of how we want the world to be. Lights On!

"Be the change you wish to see in the world."
                                                    ~Mahatma Gandhi

---

How Do You Show Up?

Have you observed how some event can happen and one person responds negatively, as if everything impacted only that person in her own "me—me—me—self" world? Yet another person's response is entirely different, seeing a much larger view and having a response that flows from a larger, insightful understanding?

Moving to a larger mind is an "awareness process" that involves a way of understanding and responding to whatever is going on. It is a way of relating (of being in relation to) the big picture. In business we like to say that one can visualize the big picture as well as the details. That's an important quality for interpersonal relationships—and getting the job done effectively.

Stephen Covey, in his book, *The 7 Habits of Highly Effective People* (1990, New York, Simon & Schuster) shares the first habit: "Be proactive." "Develop the capacity to choose your response." Covey equates proactivity and reactivity to the large and small mind. The event happens—someone makes a cutting remark; the response follows immediately—an angry retort. *Reactivity*—no conscious ability to choose one's response: small mind. In contrast, *proactivity* is the ability to choose one's response: large mind. Covey describes this as "response-ability," or the ability to be responsible.

Is this a new philosophy for living?

No. Nearly 2500 years ago in ancient China, Confucius discovered a fundamental distinction for human living. (See *I Ching or Book of Changes*, 1967, Princeton University Press.) Confucius taught that two "person-types" dwell within each of us: the small-minded person in us, and the large-minded person in us. We can respond at any time from either of the two!

The small-minded person in us is narrow, self-seeking, driven by fear and desire, ever comparing. In small mind, we see the world in dualistic (black-and-white) terms (us vs. them, win vs. lose). *Reactive, tunnel vision, scarcity mentality, dug in, selfish,* and *rigid* are descriptive words for the small mind.

The large-minded person in us has a more expansive way of relating—seeing more of the human element, sensing a larger, abundant context, recognizing the web of people affected, viewing the consequences of actions within a larger timeframe. *Proactive, abundant mentality, encompassing,* and *flexible* are descriptive words for large mind.

Confucius saw both capacities in each of us, both the capacity for small-mindedness and the capacity for large-mindedness. He came to the insight that all of us can achieve the nobility of large-minded living. (Yes! It is our choice.)

No matter what is happening to us, (hurricanes, floods, sickness, accidents, loss, grief) we still have an important *freedom*—the capacity to recognize how we relate to what is occurring in our lives. By cultivating awareness, we realize that we are free to choose how we will understand and respond to life's events. In every moment we have the capacity to choose how we will think, what we will do, and how we will be. This is also true in the business world—no matter what upsets occur, we have the ability to choose our response.

For any situation, there will be at least two ways of relating to what is occurring—one small-minded and one large-minded. Confucius would invite us to choose the large-minded way—the *"wisdom way."*

It is not what happens to us in life, it is how we respond to what is happening that matters most!

Try this:

Try journaling for the next few weeks your responses to life's events and your experience. Example: Are you ready to let go of small-minded conversations (personal and cultural)? Are you harboring grudges? Are you ready to put your gossiping aside? Are you ready to stop the cattiness? Can you move toward positive thoughts and actions? Could you have behaved differently, more maturely, for a more constructive outcome? Could you have been more open to new ideas, to doing things differently?

Helping people to move from smaller to larger mind is something we all can do. We can lift up the positive. We can present the larger context. We can find the larger-minded response. We can show up large, or we can show up small.

It is also what deep training in leadership and personal growth and development is all about. It's about making conscious response choices with our high-beam Lights On!

Adapted from: John G. Sullivan, PhD, "Small Mind, Big Mind," Meridians, *Spring 1996.*

Moment of Truth

"No one can make you feel inferior without your consent."
~*Eleanor Roosevelt*

I asked a female intern pastor (whose focus was on young adult ministry) about her words for counseling young women—especially when she thought back to her own young adult experience. Her answer was that she can see very clearly now that she erroneously put too much emphasis on what she thought other people thought about her—her appearance, her weight, her brains, her likeability, etc., and as a result, she had many lonely struggles with self-deprecation—trying to lift herself up when others put her down and trying to *fit in* to what she perceived she needed to do or be, simply because of what others conveyed. She had not been *true to herself.* Sound familiar?

This wonderful young woman went on to share that an essential part of her work is helping women to understand that self-esteem is nurtured by each of us, and *by choice*—whether women are in their teens, their 20s, 30s, 40s, 50s, 60s, 70s, 80s, or beyond. This knowledge is paramount: happiness is our birthright, and it is within each of us—a secret that so many women miss learning, for a host of reasons. This influential minister knows it is never too late to reclaim and rebuild one's personal truth.

With snide remarks and negative teardowns being so prevalent within interpersonal relationships today in social settings, political arenas, families, and in our work world, I'm reminded of my Catechism class teachings not to belittle, slander, or backbite another, but rather, to put the most charitable construction on all that others do. That lesson has served me well. So does *Do unto others as you'd have them do unto you.* And throughout my journey, I've fully learned firsthand about the *dualities of life*—I know that positives and negatives are out there—waiting to either contribute to or to diminish my self-esteem—*if I choose to let them*!

One young woman I've coached shared her repetitive life tape-recording, which began as a grade school story of "not being liked." She knew that several classmates didn't like her. She couldn't see that there were countless other classmates and teachers who did like her. Instead of thinking about the many classmates who liked her, who smiled at her, who invited her to play at recess, or the teacher who gave her a gold star—all who were positive toward her—for some reason she, instead, fixated on the negative, taking this *unlikeability* inside her core as if it were truth. She essentially treated the positives that were equally around her as neutral in meaning. Soon, she unknowingly reinforced that not-being-liked feeling every time she had another negative classmate encounter. She kept choosing to take in the negative, and it was hurtful to believe that she was unlikeable. It didn't have to be that way then, and it doesn't have to be that way now. We choose what to take in, whether to accept the negatives or the positives, or some of each!

My dad had a great saying whenever I nurtured some criticism of my work, or of my person. He'd say, "Take it in long enough to figure out whether there is a grain of truth somewhere; if so, learn from that kernel of truth, but be sure that you whisk all the rest of it away really quick, because all that's left is only chaff for the wind."

As a high-functioning, aware adult, you learn this: your happiness, joy, and self-love comes from inside of you. You know that you will never find that happiness, joy, and self-love or have it sustained from others. You are dependent on yourself.

The well of happiness comes from within, so why would we choose to let in what contaminates?

Your self-esteem depends on *your* choices. You learn that you do not have to take in the negativity that others thrust at you. You can deflect the mental and emotional poison darts if you choose. You don't have to take others' words and actions and make them your truth. You can put up your shield to those negative words and deeds and stay true to your own self, to your own inner knowledge and self-love. What makes our world so special is that we have this "free will to choose…always."

The negatives that are thrown at us are deeply gripping. They hurt because they penetrate and bruise the ego. In the world of Human Resource Management, it is often stated that just one negative "ahh shit" cancels out a dozen positive "atta-girls."

Think about this: *Life's positives are always there. Life's negatives are always there.* Which are you looking for? Which do you want to take in and which do you choose to allow in? Which do you whisk by? Which boost your self esteem? On which are you putting your attention? Which do you accept the majority of the time?

Lights On!

Postscript: I lift up these concerns: check out the bookstore shelves for the prominence of books on the subject of self-esteem. Why is it that society, communities, do-gooder groups, schools, churches, families, and psychology groups seem to lack an organized teaching approach for conveying basic self-esteem 101 knowledge and transcending learning to our young children—when they and their psyches are at such formative stages in their development? Why is it that this learning that "we each choose what we accept into ourselves" is hit-and-miss in our generational learning—even though it is so crucial to how we could better live our ensuing lives? How can females more readily learn this at a very young age and not spend the majority of their years struggling to find their self-love? Ladies...we've got big work to do with and for our children and grandchildren! If we are the hand that still rocks the cradle, then we've got some positive rocking to do and self-love how-tos to teach our young.

It's All in the *Conversation*

H ave you ever heard a word or a phrase surface in a new or different way, and subsequently hear it again and again in different-yet-familiar ways? I can recall a number of years ago, when the word "transparent" became a business buzzword. This new idea was transparent, or that task was transparent, or the hidden agenda was becoming transparent. Transparency was important!

What about the word *conversation*? Over the last few months, I've heard or read about *conversation* particularly in the realms of personal authenticity, quality relationships, and deep, meaningful interactions. It has entered my perception many times and in these interesting ways:

- People who practice Appreciative Inquiry (lifting up the positive) are familiar with "initiating *conversations of consequence.*" This is more than a strategy—it is a conscious choice and pursuit. It means no more empty conversations! It means being present!

- In a Learning Event of The Center for Self-Organizing Leadership, Inc., there were discussions on the importance of the continuous conversation and the importance of conversations of meaning and relevance.

- My daughter recently added to the enjoyment of a long road trip by bringing with her a book on conversation starters that tickled the mind and helped all of us get to know each other even better. The personal responses were delightful. Yet at the same time, deeper connections were forming.

Many have written about the importance of authentic conversations, specifically that the conversation actually *is* the barometer of the relationship. The relationship essentially can be identified, deepened or lessened, or improved or negated by the degree of authenticity we bring to our conversations. We all know the difference between a superficial conversation and a powerful, authentic one.

Author Susan Scott challenges the individual—you, me. She writes, *"On the personal note: What's the conversation out there with your name on it? The one you've been avoiding for days, weeks, months, years? Who is it with and what's the topic?"* She also challenges an organization's leadership *to hold the long-overdue conversation.* Can you imagine what great achievements could come forth if every supervisor and team leader, asked the people in their organizations and teams, *"What is the most important thing we should be talking about today?"* Can you imagine what progress could happen if everyone was involved in advancing the intentions and work of the organization as a whole? Can you imagine the increased productivity and coherence that could happen if the elephants in the room and the undiscussables were genuinely lifted up and resolved? What if you raised this same question with your family at the dinner table and were open to really listening and authentically engaging?

Some of the most important conversations you hold in life are the ones that you hold with yourself. Have you noticed your self-talk lately? How is it influencing your choices? Do you hear limiting statements like "I can't" or "Yes...but"? Are you retreating into yourself or facing yourself head on? What if the next conversation you had with yourself started this way? *"Self...what is the most important thing we should be talking about today?"* And, tell the truth—speak directly to the heart of the issue. *Ahh...conversations that transform!*

Recommended reading: Meg Wheatley's book, Turning to One Another: Simple Conversations to Restore Hope to the Future *underscores the centrality of conversation in healing everything from personal relationships to organizational dysfunction to world discord.*

Susan Scott's book, Fierce Conversations...Achieving Success at Work & in Life, One Conversation at a Time.

Choice!

*C*hoice has been a resounding word for me lately, and the phrase *by choice* (of one's own volition) seems to resonate too.

In just the few hours I've been up and about today, I've made numerous choices. That is, I have selected or made a decision when faced with two or more possibilities. Here are some examples from today: to take a longer-than-usual morning walk, to have strawberries *and* bananas at breakfast, to deep clean the tile floors with my steam-cleaning machine, to make a very difficult personal phone call, and to end my procrastination—carving out the time to consciously put pen to paper about this word, *choice.*

Think about all the choices you make in your current life—from the superficial choices to ones with deeper meaning, to ones that involve others, to ones that have life-changing impact.

During the course of a Lights On! Workshop©, I asked a group of women to each think deeply about important and critical choices made in their personal lives. What was that pivotal point? What difference did that choice make? How did just one choice co-create her future? Was there a strong life-principle present that anchored that choice?

The important learning to me, about choice, is that we all have it! And we all have it in equal measure. We each have 24 hours a day to *deliberately* choose, to co-create our own lives for the better.

Barry Schwartz, in *The Paradox of Choice*, notes that every choice we make is a testament to our autonomy, to our sense of self-determination.

Dee Wallace, in her book, *Conscious Creation*, underscores that we are all creating. Every thought, belief, and action (choice) is a creation, but most of us are not creating consciously. Creating and living out our lives is an ongoing process—one in which our choices do matter—one wherein we must be conscious (aware) of our thoughts, our beliefs, our fears, and our wants. Essentially, she notes, we are always "at choice."

I like that—*at choice!* Lights On!

Who Is This Person? Is That Really Me? Which Me?

My husband and I returned home from a long work trip just before Thanksgiving. We had some leisure sightseeing time built into those travels too. Since we've returned, we've been reminiscing via digital photos and computer slide show.

There is one photo in particular that I cannot bear to gaze upon. I asked, "Is that really me?" If it is really me, then I have to concern myself with a deeper question as to what has happened to me. How did I come to look like that?

Have you had a similar experience?

I've come to the conclusion that I must comprise *several selves— mostly contradictory.* That is, I'm like an octopus, with multiple tentacles. For example, which of my many selves decided it is okay to munch from the M&Ms in the candy jar each time I pass by it? It certainly can't be the same self that decided that thin was in! It can't be the same self that decided to do the crunches on the exercise/rowing machine. Which one is making my snack selections? Chances are it isn't the same one that wants to be healthy. How do I get my many selves all believing (again) in the same program? It would be good if I could get this figured out...*before I step on the scale again.*

Cognitive dissonance theory provides some great clues. Cognitive dissonance is that uncomfortable feeling caused by holding two contradictory ideas simultaneously. It is when one's beliefs and one's behaviors don't match up. Either I'll have to change my behavior with the M&Ms (to get in synch with the belief that I need to eat healthy), or I have to change what I believe to match the unhealthy behaviors (at my age, with my genes, this is how it is, and a few M&Ms won't make much difference).

Psychologists note that we have higher-order selves and lower-order selves that provoke these contradictions. While it is our higher-order selves that commit to long-term goals, it is a mixture of lower-order selves that have the task of accomplishing the goals and reconciling our actions. (My spirit is willing, but my body is weak!)

So the task is to align them; and in the case of my M&Ms, it is the lower-level behavior that I need to bring up to a worthier, more noble place!

To solve such contradictory dilemmas, and to advance your deliberate, developmental growth, you have to *consciously activate* a higher-order self. The moment you begin to observe your own thoughts, you begin to operate from a higher-order self. So why not create a mental model of what you'd really like to see happen and visualize it over and over again throughout the day and definitely (in my case) when walking by the M&Ms? It is the process of creating a clear picture of your intention (whatever that might be), seeing it clearly throughout your day, then seizing it again and again until it has been raised enough to reflect both your belief and your in-synch behaviors. Psychologists call this *intentional self-creation practice.*

Hmmmmm.

I would guess that removing the M&M jar would be an alternative way for me to promote this alignment. (Remove the temptation). But that would be too easy. That would be pandering to my lower-order self. No, I want to fulfill my higher-order self's development; I choose to ignore the M&Ms because I'd rather not have the calories. I have a vision of health. But I'll need to have a lot of post-it notes posted around to help me see, grasp, and adopt the higher-order self I'm trying to become (at least as it applies to chocolate!).

Here's to whatever works for you to align your beliefs and behaviors. May they match up beautifully! Lights On!

The Dots Do Connect!

One of the first college courses I took was on human development through the lifespan. I loved this course. For me, it was the right course at the right time.

Essentially, this course explored the human journey from birth to death. It examined the physical development, the cognitive (intellectual) growth, and the emotional (even spiritual) development as we live our entire lives. I learned about the physicality of babies, teenagers, adults, and centenarians. I learned about the egocentrism of teens and the increased seeking of meaning and purpose as we move forward in our lives. I learned about our innate need to grow, to develop, and to strive forward.

The course focused first on the individual, then the family, the community, the nation, and the world. We examined socioeconomic factors; we charted generations; we looked at patterns of behavior and recalled world civilizations. We delved into the macro and micro, and always at the core was the evolving person! I was fascinated as we connected the dots, linking personhood to each developmental element and to sharing with other humans something more than a point in time. Yes, the dots linked to something larger than oneself.

So why did this course speak to me so strongly? I was 45 when I obtained my Bachelor of Science degree in Business Management and Economics. I'd pursued this degree while I worked full-time, was married, and was caring for my daughter. Yet it wasn't because I was a nontraditional student that I found it so important.

This course wholly affirmed for me that I had chosen the correct career path. I was on the right track and had been all along. Hallelujah! I loved people and working with people. At that time I was a Human Resources Manager; people and problem solving were my business. It was a role that I certainly enjoyed and for which I was well recognized. But this one course enabled me to verbalize why my life's work was following this path and why this path was the right one!

For me, it is not just about people, it is about knowing people, understanding people, caring about people, and being able to connect the dots between the various aspects of their lives. It is about the why and the what and the how and the when of their lives. (Repeat...their lives, not my life.) It is about being able to discuss that which might otherwise go by unknown or undervalued.

Each person is as large and as full as their lifespan experience. Yet so many people never bother to get past the first superficial layers of communicating to find that fullness. This is the challenge that excites me! (I know that every employee complaint, every grievance, every turf battle is better resolved when the examination has gone deep, and when the who, what, how, why, and so what questions have been fully answered.)

Yes, I reaffirmed that every person, no matter at what phase of their life, has an important story to share. And when you genuinely ask someone to share the story that's in their heart and on their mind—when you can sense what it is that makes them tick, you can't help but notice that "signature flourish" that's theirs to hold and yours to discover!

For me, that's what being a people person—a real, caring HR Manager—means! Yes, the dots have always been connected! The question is how deep into my own dot matrix was I willing to delve? Was I willing to see and embrace my path? To keep moving forward? To see that every step along the way was perfect for my growth, for approaching this moment?

Take a deep look at how your life's dots connect one to another. I'll wager that your dot-connection journey (encompassing where you've been, what you've learned, along with your myriad experiences) makes for a beautiful story. Your story. How deep into your dot matrix are you willing to delve? Are you ready to see that everything in your life has been evolving perfectly? Everything, all along, has encompassed the perfect next steps, next growing experiences, for your evolution.

"It is an ancient story, yet it is ever new." ~Heinrich Heine

"We dance round in a ring and suppose, but the Secret sits in the middle and knows." ~Robert Frost

The Present Moment Is Now!

"Life is not about how to survive the storm, but how to dance in the rain." ~Unattributed

Mindfulness is an important practice. Meditation is an important practice. To be quiet, to be still, to hear the intuitive voice within, to connect with your God/Source/Creator, to know your deep breath—all this brings you into the present moment. Being in the present moment is not easy for adults. Yet, as children, we were well-acquainted with the present moment, with "what is now." As adults, we have to learn (again) how to connect with our Source—how to breathe, to go within, to reconnect, to experience where you are in this moment.

Colleagues have asked me what I know about "present moment thinking." I struggle too. One book, *The Power of Now* by Elkhart Tolle was, for me, a difficult read. Yet this is the sort of book that tends to swirl around one's mind for a while; life's events resonate with new questions, and different thinking comes forth. There were several gems of information that seemed very important for my journey. These excerpts are what stood out the most for me:

Unease, anxiety, tension, stress, worry, and concerns you harbor are all forms of *fear and scarcity mentality*, and are caused by living with *too much future* and *not enough presence*. Get into the *now.*

Guilt, regret, resentment, grievances, sadness, bitterness, indignation, and scorn are all forms of *non-forgiveness*, and are caused by living with *too much past* and *not enough presence*. Get into the *now.*

When you are full of problems, when your life is moving at a frantic high pace, there is no room for anything new to enter, no room for a solution. So whenever you can, make some room; create some space so that you find the life underneath your situation. Getting quiet, finding stillness, and listening to your breath are all important. *(Be still, and hear my voice!)*

No matter what happens to you (and, yes, as you are human, you must live your life, so you will sometimes encounter very difficult situations), the learning remains that it is important to recognize the need to make a simple choice, a simple *now* decision in those moments; it is about facing and embracing what is *now* before you.

If you find your here-and-now (career, family, interpersonal situation) intolerable and it makes you deeply unhappy—you have several options:

1. Remove yourself from the situation. (You can flee a situation—that is a choice. It's known as the flight syndrome when the circumstances are such that you cannot continue, you fully recognize the consequences of removing yourself, and you are willing to take responsibility for this action.)

2. Ignore it. (Let it go—emotionally, physically, and intellectually. It is what it is. Don't put any more stress or energy into it. Move on.)

3. Change it. Do what you can to address the situation and make it better. (You are response-able.)

4. Accept it totally. That means that you surrender to the fact that this really is the situation and you are experiencing what you are experiencing. You feel the emotion. You may not like it; you do not condone what has happened or the

119

behaviors surrounding it, but you choose to accept that this situation is yours at this moment, fair or unfair. You breathe it in, and then you breathe it out. You totally let go of all the judgment around it. You put aside all resistance. You release all emotion. (Hard to do…but this is what accepting it totally means.) You own the situation, finding some piece of constructive learning in it for you, personally. You realize that this situation is not yours to change, but that you are to let it be, to let God/Source/Creator work with this in a larger timeframe. You allow it, be with it for that moment, and then you let it go (fully), and move on, not to revisit again—all negativity released.

If you want to take responsibility for your life at such decision points, you must choose one of those options, and you must choose *now*. Then you must accept the consequences. No excuses. No negativity. No carryover to grumble over another day. Whatever your decision is—whether to leave it, to ignore it, to change it, or to accept it—there is a big caveat: *You must drop all the negativity first.* If you choose to accept it, then accept it totally by dropping all the inner resistance. Submit to it. No more wallowing. It's over, so let it be over. Move your attention and focus to something constructive, something positive in this moment, and something for which you are grateful. *Being grateful is the quickest way to see the gift in anything and the quickest way to connect with God/Source/Creator.* See everything in your life as a gift from the Divine.

I'm reminded again of the "now wisdom" of the Serenity Prayer:

"God, grant me the serenity to accept the things I cannot change, the courage to change the things I can, and the wisdom to know the difference."

Recommended Reading: The Power of Now *by Elkhart Tolle, 1999, New World Library.*

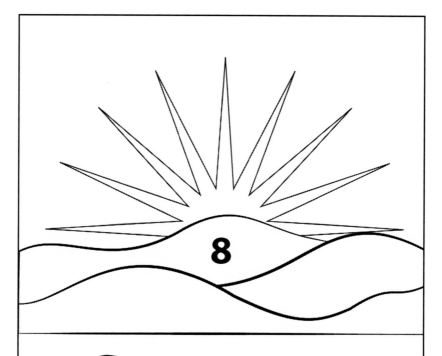

8

COURAGE TO BECOME

Angel in the Marble

"I saw the angel in the marble and carved until I set him free."
~Michelangelo

Each of us has some Michelangelo in us. We are forever striving to bring that confident, beautiful self into full form. We spend our lives knowingly or unknowingly trying to become that which we are intended to be.

If you happened to be one of the attendees at any of the showings of The GLOW Project movie, you understand. Each of us has a powerful being inside of us; each of us has a "glow" to radiate. We each have to find that glow—to release that "angel in the marble." All the while, we are living our lives, with all the ups and downs.

Being released from those marble constraints involves discovering one's passion and living according to what matters most. Psychologists tell us that our "constant striving" focuses on five different, interrelated life strategies, each of which includes an emotional barometer. Each is actively present every day, in every moment—always tugging. And each invokes one's next action.

They are:

Competency	Feeling Successful (or not)
Usefulness	Feeling Needed (or not)
Belonging	Feeling Valued (or not)
Potency	Feeling Empowered (or not)
Optimism	Feeling Hopeful (or not)

When you awoke this morning, how were you feeling in each of these arenas?

Think for a moment about your lowest lows, and your highest highs. Which of the above strategies was most impacted? Think about who or what in your life most helps you or hinders you in these five categories. Sometimes one arena can be hugely impacted (for example, being demoted) and your sense of competency, your sense of feeling successful, will take a nose dive. Conversely, you may learn that you are being promoted and provided a bonus—so your sense of competency surges upward! Or you might be experiencing the "empty nest syndrome" and you are feeling pangs of not being very needed or valued. Or you may be experiencing great loss and your sense of optimism is deeply impacted.

What happens when you experience a negative in any of the above categories? Immediately you begin to strive to find a positive in that arena and/or to find balance via one or more of the other arenas. While you might sulk for a bit over being demoted, you'll ultimately be beckoned forward to look to increase your competence—to find something different wherein you again can feel successful. (For example, when I retired from the corporate world I had to reinvent myself; I had to become competent, useful, and potent in another realm. In my case, that was in consulting and coaching.)

Whenever you experience the negative in any of these arenas, you are internally beckoned to seek another positive, to achieve balance at the minimum, and to ultimately move towards emotional joy. *But wouldn't it be great if you could stack your deck with more positives than negatives to begin with?* That's where releasing your angel from the marble by living your passion and capitalizing on your gifts enriches your treasure trove and provides a leg up on emotional joy.

The psychological riddle to releasing your "angel in the marble" is that the more you understand your gifts and live your passion, the more you'll find yourself feeling positive in all five of these life-strategy categories. And the more positive-feeling you become, the more you knowingly and purposely continue to act in ways that increase your positivity in these five life strategy arenas even more—all the while, your angel continues to come forth, radiating with that "glow."

Michelangelo saw the glow in his masterpieces and had to carve. We see the glow in ourselves and have to act! Lights On!

Is That All There Is?

This is the title of a hit ballad from 1969. The artist was the sultry singer, Peggy Lee. The song's lyrics are based on Thomas Mann's short fiction story "Disillusionment." The song title is intended to reach deep into one's soul; it reflects the personal quest—the search for meaning for our lives.

At a deep level we know—particularly as the years go by—that something is calling us. We crave wholeness, completeness, and individuation. We experience an "awakening to this deep need." Some of us may embrace this time of awakening. It is an invitation, a calling, a soft whisper in our heart, a nudge, a stimulus for us to *become*—to live more deeply, more passionately, more honestly, more in tune with the dance of life and the music inside us.

Carl Jung defined this point in life (usually about midlife, but for some it occurs much sooner) as a time of strong spiritual growth. It is a time of intense change. As our menses fade, as our need for procreation ends, as a career and/or family-anchoring no longer envelops us, as one becomes more secure, we turn toward concerns about the essential meaning of life. And it is true that with aging bodies we do glimpse our mortality. With end of life in the field of vision comes a clarifying of our life purpose, our relationships, our life path. We want our lives to have meant something, to have stood for something more than the hyphen on the grave marker, or a sequencing in the strands of DNA.

Interestingly, some who are confronting this confusing transition-time-of-life experience a loss of identity: sometimes divorce/separation, empty nest syndrome, anxiety, depression, boredom, hopelessness, or emptiness. They ask, "Is that all there is?" So Peggy Lee's song title has found a receptive audience— the words are hauntingly resonant for many women, particularly at midlife. Some commence this time of life through a sudden dramatic crisis. Others will notice subtle shifts in their feelings and needs, their choices, and their goals. Others sleepwalk. For some, the turmoil can upset a well-ordered world and threaten their sense of identity. There is a deepening need for finding new expressions of self. Can one navigate through this inner confusion and upheaval? Yes! Absolutely!

At the heart of the transition is the letting go of who we are in order to become who we are supposed to be. We tune in to our intuitive nature; we listen for guidance. We seek. We face our courage issues. We transform. We become—like the butterfly—emergent, open to change, open to new opportunities. This awakening time provides a unique opportunity for growth and change. We have the opportunity to integrate the knowledge gained during this transition to deeply enrich the next segments of our lives. We become empowered. We move forward. We emerge anew.

This is a time when the unlived parts of the self come to the forefront. It is a time when we know that we are more than the mask we show to others. The poet Robert Bly notes that we spend half our lives putting parts of ourselves into the shadow and the other half trying to take them out again. It is a time when "our intuitive knowing" is keen.

So is this transformation and calling at midlife new? No. We have been called to this place of renewal and change for generations. Joseph Campbell has popularized the notion of the Hero's Journey, including the call to adventure, separation, questing, and a return—always returning transformed. Similar archetypal examples of this awakening and transformation exist in stories across cultures. This part of the journey, though, has a natural pathway with a secret affirmation for those who travel on the quest. The secret is the answer to the question, "Is That All There Is?" The answer is "No, that is not all there is…this new dance-set in life is just beginning, and there are more steps awaiting your joy. You just have to answer the invitation, answer your inner call to step forward!"

Recommended reading: Awakening at Midlife, *by Kathleen Brehony, PhD. Her book is an important read for one's journey.*

Self-Discovery

"Life isn't about finding yourself. Life is about creating yourself!"
~George Bernard Shaw

Is this the time in your life for discovering your authentic self? To know who you really are? To make the choices that will move you along a greater or different path? Is destiny calling you?

- What are you doing differently at this time of your life? What are you *becoming*?

- Do you see the possibilities?

- Do you have a vision? a map? a plan?

- Do you have the courage to consciously *become*? It takes courage to *become.*

What is meant by *becoming?* It means making any change from the lower level of potentiality to the higher level of actuality. It demands action...action that only you can take for yourself.

Moving-forward actions are sometimes difficult. Interestingly, though, we are not alone—we've got lots of company for this journey!

There is a strong likelihood that somewhere within the 40-55 age timeframe (the menopausal years), a woman will be shaken deeply, perhaps to her very core. For a variety of reasons, she may find herself in a period of heightened vulnerability. Some call this timeframe the midlife crisis time. In Greek, the root word for *crisis* is *krinein*—meaning a turning point, or a separating, a division. Webster's dictionary defines *crisis* as a turning point, a decisive moment. Indeed, one might conclude that the decisiveness needed at this time of a woman's life is about letting go, changing, separating from that which needs to be left behind, and pivoting—actually looking forward to what one needs next in one's *becoming,*

"The truth is that women actually blossom, rather than fade, at midlife." ~Stephanie Marston

---

In my own coaching business, Lights On! Workshop©, I find that there are recurrent themes raised by the women I've coached—including some in their early 30s. Some are overwhelmed with the negative side of life (emptiness, lingering life struggles—not knowing how to break the patterns or how to set healthy boundaries). Others sense the magnitude of life's transitions and the inner calling of deeper, more subtle nudges to move forward. They feel compelled to move forward using different paths. Many are looking for a way to clarify their vision about life, career, family, community, and personal causes. Many wish to see and to follow their personal roadmap with more clarity. Midlife provides the wake-up call, an attentive time for re-evaluating, a time when you can become the person you have always wanted to be. This is the time of personal dreams fulfilled. This is the time when new opportunities burst forth—they are yours if you will seize them!

Sometime during midlife, women tend to awaken and come full circle; they assume personal responsibility for their own *becoming,* for their fulfillment. Many life events can evoke this change—loss of a spouse, divorce, empty nest, career changes, desire for deeper education, deeper meditation, a desire to give back to the community, new hobbies, new interests, or a connection to a deep cause that resonates from within. Where previously they may have gifted themselves to their children, family, and/or career in multiple roles, now the emphasis is shifted—inward. This is the time of rebirth and renewal, of blossoming forth (first from within, then outward again)—when women are comfortable enough to step forward and claim their own ideas, recognize their personal zest and enthusiasm, their unique sense of adventure, and their spirit of renewed vitality. This is the call to the authentic life.

"Now is the time to recognize an authentic self. Now is the time to create a future brimming with tremendous possibilities—and make midlife the richest, most profound and satisfying years of all." ~Stephanie Marston, If Not Now, When?: Reclaiming Ourselves at Midlife

Why Are We (Women) Always Seeking Permission?

I was with two colleagues, having coffee and conversation. The subject easily moved from a superficial exchange of niceties to the politics of our respective workplaces. One colleague, whose career path challenges have been within a male-dominated industry, began to share how she'd recently had a performance review; she'd been told *she just wasn't assertive enough.* Yuck! (We knew that *lack of assertiveness* certainly wasn't an appropriate label for our friend.) That led to a lively conversation of what this world would be like *if it were a matriarchal society.* Our conversation circled back to the present. We questioned why it is that Fortune 500 top earners remain primarily men and why it is that gender pay equity remains a common conference theme? *What is it that is still holding women back?*

I found this question hugely provocative, especially having lived through the 60s and having been part of the fight for fairness for women in the workplace (and life) for decades. How would you answer the question of specifically *what* is holding women back from making huge strides in the workplace?

Would you answer…*because we are still waiting for permission?* Many women are doing exactly that—waiting for permission. How do I know? I did a Google search for "women waiting for permission." After 10 pages of website entries, I quit reading. Instead, I ruminated on recurring themes:

- You are conditioned to think that you need to honor someone else's wishes, so you put your own dreams on hold. Why is that? Is that noble? Thank goodness that this latest generation of younger women is willing to stand up and say, "I'll give some here…but I'm not giving you everything I've got! I've got to fulfill my own life!"

- Women tend to love and to give everything, putting themselves last. You are the last one to eat, the last one to go to bed, the last one out the door. Why is that? Is that because that's what grandmother did? And your mother too? Thank goodness there's a move toward sharing the household chores; there's no such word as *superwoman* anymore!

- You define yourself in terms of relationships to other people (what your spouse/significant other or parents or children might think or want), so you'll make them happy as opposed to yourself. You think either/or, instead of both/and...why is that? Is it because giving to others is so good? Is it the magnanimous thing to do? Is it because it is expected by society? Is that how you expect your daughter to be?

- You need permission to invest in yourself. Why do you seek that nod of approval first? Do you not know that an investment in yourself is a worthy one? Who's creating the pecking order here?

- You need permission to take the next step, to move ahead, or to speak what you know is right. Why do you hesitate to raise your hand? To step forward? To advance yourself? What are you waiting for? Are you afraid you might do something wrong? Are you afraid you might be criticized? Are you afraid that someone else might not like what you have to say or what you are doing? Are you being less assertive than you could be just so that you do not create conflict? Why must you have certainty before you act?

- As women, we are natural caretakers. We want to make the people around us happy and the world a better place— often at the expense of ourselves. That desire for harmony is strong—sometimes stronger than our need to assert our personal selves.

I concur that many women genuinely do have trouble giving themselves *permission* to move forward. They'll often wait for everything to be lined up first—they're looking for 100% guarantees. They hold themselves back, giving a host of excuses. They just keep that dialog going on and on with themselves, which hinders forward action. They hesitate—wanting assurances for taking responsibility for a decision. They look to others to affirm themselves, their thinking, and their actions. They're timid about standing out, about being different, about being labeled *assertive*. Are you one of them? What about your treatment of other women who are trying to move forward assertively? Are you able to praise the success of other women? Or are you contributing to their demise? Think about that!

Sometimes I think that as women, in general, we don't even think about our *personal power*. Also, that we, as women, have an *unconscious habit* of needing permission to excel, let alone to influence our outcomes. It's like we're waiting for the cheerleading squad to come out and cheer us on, rather than running full speed ahead because it is the right thing to do... in the now. It seems that we're waiting for someone to say "it's okay, it's your turn now."

I believe that Suzanne Evans, a marketing expert and creator of *Be The Change Event*, phrased the question best:

"Is it possible that we have such a distinct female biology and neurological need to seek and receive approval, that we'll always have difficulty getting beyond this permission-thing?"

Not if I can help it! I didn't ask for or wait for permission to wear pantsuits in the corporate office (back in the '60s when skirts and dresses were the expected norm); I didn't wait for permission to become a leader in the corporate world; and I'm certainly not waiting for permission to move forward now. I didn't seek permission to start my business, or write my book, or offer up speaking engagements. The world is hungry for my gifts...I need not wait for permission to excel, to have, to do, or to be!

The same applies to you.

Here's to permission to *not* need permission!

Why Women Hang Back

I was recently a speaker at a Gender Pay Equity Conference. One of the threads weaving through it was that women, in general, lack confidence in negotiating pay as they enter the workforce, and thereafter, women have difficulty in creating upward mobility within their respective work organizations. Ultimately, and overall, these tendencies contribute to the continuing gap in relative compensation.

In a larger framework, it has been my experience (in 30 years of working within a large organization and 10+ years in coaching women in many walks of life) that many women lack basic managerial courage (command skills, conflict management, confronting appropriately, being able to stand alone and strong, being able to take criticism and turn it into a learning opportunity). Negotiation is part of this managerial courage—it is a life-important and life-long skill. Please note that my statement is not meant to paint all women with this same brush. Nor is this exclusive to the female gender; I've also met men in the workplace who lack managerial courage. Some characteristics that demonstrate a lack of basic managerial courage include: crisis-avoiding; wishy-washy—unable to take a stand; fear of criticism/failure; unable to take the heat—uncomfortable being grilled; defensive—low risk-takers—not liking uncertainty; defensive—in the face of complaints; not being open to criticism; and an unwillingness to learn from criticism. *I've found that within the business world that finding one's managerial courage, one's self, one's voice, one's command center is key!*

When it comes to negotiations, here are some general tendencies to consider:

- Women tend to view fewer situations as even involving a negotiation. They thus just accept what's offered, or what is, more often than men, and don't question it or even ask for more.

- Women tend to have lower expectations and self-confidence than men in many negotiation settings and thus, when they do ask, they tend to ask for less and concede more.

- Women tend to experience higher anxiety than men in conflict-oriented negotiation settings.

- Women's tendency to be more relationship-oriented and cooperative can give them an advantage in situations where the parties recognize the value of the relationships and a more collaborative negotiation environment exists.

- Women, when negotiating on behalf of others, seem to do that better than when seeking something more for themselves individually.

- Women tend to expect that co-workers, bosses, and people in general will automatically be fair, that most situations should not even include the need for a negotiation.

- Women tend to play win-win more often; whereas, men in the workplace tend to play win-lose. As women, we are natural caretakers—we want to make the people around us happy and the world a better place; we often do this by ignoring or neglecting our own needs.

- Women, in general, are natural at nurturing. Women seek harmony. Women tend to want to appease, for the sake of finding that harmony. Dealing with conflict is difficult. So sometimes ending the conflict is more important than staying in the heat long enough to get the best result.

Why do these tendencies exist?

They generally derive from society's expectations and social conditioning—from childhood on—of the different gender-oriented traits and roles. Women are thought to be more other-oriented, and men are thought to be more self-oriented. Men seek power; women seek community.

So what do these tendencies have to do with courage? With command skills? Especially when trying to succeed in the mixed-gender workplace?

Being able to hold the important and difficult conversations is essential to overcoming courage issues. I learned to stand strong very early in my life, having taken charge over many areas of my household while I was still in high school. Responsibility was and is my middle name! My years in a career at DuPont provided me many opportunities to learn, to grow, to develop, to hone my management and leadership skills, and to build my business acumen. Yet, when Susan Scott wrote *Fierce Conversations: Achieving Success at Work and in Life, One Conversation at a Time*, I ordered copies for many a woman colleague. I read the book from cover to cover, then I took her course! Fierce conversations does not mean "mean"; rather, it means "robust, intense, strong, powerful, passionate, eager, unbridled." I highly recommend it to learn to personally and professionally *act with courage, care, and confidence (one conversation at a time).* And this is precisely what successful women have learned to do in the workplace — you can learn to *act—in spite of your fears!*

Courage issues:

To me, having managerial courage means being able to stand up and appropriately, maturely, and diplomatically say what needs to be said at the right time, to the right person, in the right manner, with the right impact. It means not being afraid to take negative action when necessary. It means facing up to people and work problems in any situation quickly and directly. Can you muster this courage? What about supporting other women? When a woman in your workplace has mustered the courage to stand tall, do you chime in with support? Or do you wither?

There is an inspiring book by Birute Regine that is wonderfully titled, *Iron Butterflies: Women Transforming Themselves and the World*. This book speaks volumes about how many successful women have dealt with vulnerability in themselves, within the workplace. *Iron Butterflies* convincingly demonstrates how traditional feminine skills and values—inclusion, empathy, relational awareness, emotional strength, and seeking a holistic perspective—can be applied to empower more people than ever before. Like the many women profiled, leaders in the twenty-first century will paradoxically embrace vulnerability and durability to create better working and living relationships for us all.

These women, the Iron Butterflies, also possess managerial courage. How wonderful that we have such strong women role models. How wonderful that we have Iron Butterflies from whom we can learn! Here's to building courage! Lights On!

The Gift of Christmas Courage

Christmas Eve was the most exciting night of the year for us, growing up in a small German-American village in Western New York. Even though we were poor, we didn't know it. There would be at least one or two packages wrapped and waiting for each of us to open once we returned home from Christmas Eve candlelight church services.

Our little village was the kind of place where everyone knew each other—there were no secrets. Most of us were actually related to each other in some way. This Christmas, 1957, would prove to be a pivotal point in my life. The snow was already on the ground. The holiday wreaths, lit trees, and decorated cookies added to the anticipation. My siblings and I were excited. That is, we were as excited as we could be living in a household with a mentally and emotionally unstable mother where anything could happen.

Our parochial school classes had been practicing for weeks to present our Christmas Eve program. I was to sing a solo that night, and I was ready! The morning of Christmas Eve Day, however, I awoke to pandemonium, including police and ambulance sirens. While we had been sleeping throughout the night, our Mom had slipped out of the house and begun knocking on the doors of townspeople, dressed only in her nightgown, and making schizophrenic pronouncements that would still be talked about decades later. Her actions resulted in her being institutionalized that very day. The town was abuzz. Our family was distraught. As kids, we were totally embarrassed (the stigma attached to this couldn't be higher), and we knew how our town's gossips were telling this tale. How could I stand up and sing my solo when all I wanted to do was cry and hide from it all?

Then Dad called us all together and hugged all of us kids. He gave me an extra hug and said, "Don't worry one bit about what happened today or about what people think, or about unkind things they may be whispering. They aren't choosing to see that Mom has a sickness. We all wish that things could be different. But this is Christmas. The good Lord wants to hear you sing tonight, and he'll be listening and so will I. Stand up, hold your Christmas candle high, and show that special courage you have. Let it shine through your presence there tonight. Be who you are—you have a song to sing."

I did. I sang my 9-year-old heart out with "O Little Town of Bethlehem."

I found my inner courage that night. It was a precious life gift—a product of circumstance and a compassionate, encouraging father. This gift has served me well. My life's work has been in helping business leaders and organizations deal with tough, tangled workplace issues—all the while lifting up the good and finding coherent and courageous ways through the mire.

Note: This article was adapted from an essay originally written for and published in The Gratitude Book Project®: My Favorite Christmas Memory, *2011.*

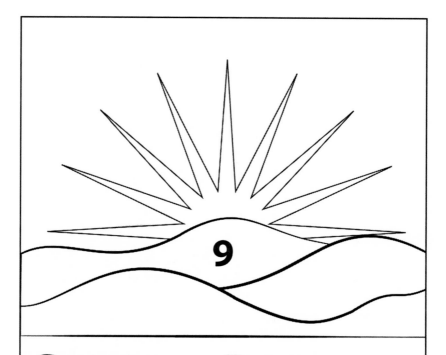

9

CHRYSALIS PARALYSIS...
STUCK IN YOUR OWN COCOON

Life Becomes Aware of You When You Become Aware of It!

Every person goes through life with some degree of awareness—some degree of clarity or knowing about what is happening to them, with them, and around them. They have some sense about crafting their life journey and critical points along their path. This awareness varies greatly—from people who seem to be sleepwalking through life, to others who are stuck and moving nowhere, to others who are very much in tune with life and life's offerings. Life's intention is that we continue to expand in our awareness as we travel our respective journeys.

I've learned not to judge a person on where they are along their respective personal journey. I may not like what they do, what they say, or how they behave; sometimes I have to bite my tongue. While I have a personal right to defend my own person—and I do—still, I need to recognize that *they may not know what they do*. I've learned that my judgment of them won't change things. I recognize, instead, *that people behave in ways that reflect their level of life experiences (negatives/positives), their circumstances, their maturity, their knowing, and their awareness or lack of awareness of their call to grow forward.* That adult person is responsible for her own behavior—and for changing it, if she so chooses, and as she decides to move forward to an enlarged vision.

Life naturally requires us to move forward as time moves forward and our aging moves forward. We move forward in the various facets of our lives—intellectually, emotionally, spiritually, physically, and in our relationships, growth, and development. When I encounter a person who has been sleepwalking (and many people stay in that mode), or when I talk with a person who is just coming to realize that there are connections in this world greater than their small world, I will share the following with them if they want to hear it. It is a means to jump-start the journey forward.

- Awareness and action. This means "consciously" being aware of the flow of life…and consciously taking actions to insert yourself into that flow of energy.

- Life has an energy, and when you allow yourself to get in with the energy flow, that is when doors open, when serendipity happens, when you meet people you are supposed to meet, when you get new insights and new answers, when new pathways open up, and when things flow smoothly—almost effortlessly. This is synchronicity.

- Here are some ways to put your personal self, your life force, into the whole of life to help get the most out of it, to let it pull you—rather than you having to "push the noodle" (force things to happen).

- List three people you know well or casually who intrigue you. Write down something that you desire to ask each person. Then make it a point to connect with them and ask them. Get more insights—build and expand your awareness. Remember that *awareness* equals *intention* (for what you choose to have, to do, or to be) plus *attention* (to what you focus or give your attention). When you've followed through with acting on your list—repeat the process. Keep your questions flowing into the mix. Participate. Your actions matter.

- List three ideas that really excite you. Is there something you should be doing about them? Write down what your first step will be. Are you compelled to act? To inquire further? To raise a question? Garner your courage to act—go with the flow of the excitement of your idea.

- Give three people positive feedback every day. Let your actions be spontaneous.

- Give yourself three pieces of positive feedback every day. Let your self-talk be nonjudgmental.

- List three times that you recently have lost yourself in what you were doing because you enjoyed it so much. What is important about those moments? When will you make some time to do more of this?

- Love and fear are on the opposite ends of the emotional spectrum. You can't feel both at the same time. So, choose love. Each day write down in a journal three things that you are truly grateful for—big or small. Dwell on the positive. Let your self-talk be personally uplifting to you. Find the positive around you. Find the positive within you.

- Do something good for someone (or for many people over the course of time) *anonymously* (like a secret pal). But keep the secret indefinitely—expect nothing in return.

- Write and send or telephone a "thank you" (card, letter, e-mail, or call) every day.

Are you flowing with life's stream? Or are you seemingly moving against the current?

It's your choice! Lights On!

"Each of us has a responsibility to pay attention and expand our own self-knowledge, to craft a sense of purpose and meaning for our lives, to articulate a set of values to guide our behavior, and to create ever-expanding visions for our lives. Each of our choices, large and small, will change our interconnected world if only in microscopic yet important ways. Do we make choices that increase the harmony in our lives and in all other life on the planet? Do we make choices that increase our learning? What do we invest our energy in? Do we live the change we want to see in the world so that our example will teach others?" ~Tom Heuerman

Setting Boundaries—Guarding against Nasty Behavior

Setting boundaries has been a topic that I'd been contemplating and researching for some time. Yet it took a situation with a colleague within a professional setting to bring it to the forefront. I knew, in dealing with this specific situation, that somehow, I was the victim; I had allowed myself to be the victim and found myself feeling bad without knowing precisely why—without being able to articulate it. I just knew that I was definitely feeling small, inferior, and very confused as to how and why the victimization unfolded. I knew I needed to address this situation.

I found the book *Nasty People: How to Stop Being Hurt by Them Without Stooping to Their Level* (Jay Carter, PhD, 2003) to be most insightful. I highly recommend this book to you—for helping to make the interactions you engage in along your life's journey better. In fact, the remainder of this article is going to sound like a book report. Essentially, it is, as I want to share Dr. Carter's important perspectives. I underscore that this is about behavior—manipulative behavior—by people whose *behavior* is labeled "nasty"; as differentiated from the person.

Have you been hurt, betrayed, degraded, demeaned, or diminished by a person whose behavior has been nasty? Perhaps it is your boss, your parent, your spouse, a sibling, a colleague, a teammate, or even someone you consider a friend. Whoever it is, he or she is an *"invalidator"*—one who feeds on your self-esteem, your self-confidence, your personal worth; one who causes confusion and uncertainty that is difficult to define; one who can cause mental anguish; one who can cause a gnawing unhappiness. You can stop being the brunt of this abuse (yes, abuse) and put an end to sneak attacks on your soul—while remaining a class act and without resorting to nasty tactics.

The theme of the book (*Nasty People*) is "*invalidation*"—a term the author uses to describe "one person injuring or trying to injure another" (consciously or subconsciously). As Dr. Carter shares, "An *invalidation* can range anywhere from a shot in the back to a *tsk, tsk* to a deep cutting remark. A rolling of the eyeballs can be invalidation and so can a punch in the nose. Yet it is usually the *sneaky invalidators* that cause the most damage. Destroying a person's capability to be whole is probably worse than any physical damage any person can do to another. Invalidators are famous for taking even small moments of happiness away from you, as in the office bully that ruins the cutting of the cake honoring a company service anniversary!"

Dr. Carter's perspective is that "*the major reason invalidation occurs so often is that it works (in the short run).*" What if the process of invalidation was exposed?

Dr. Carter goes on to say: "the big part of the cure for invalidation is achieved when we simply spot it. Remaining undetected and unchallenged is what gives invalidation its power."

If invalidation didn't work, nobody would do it! This is worth repeating. *If invalidation didn't work, nobody would do it!*

Dr. Carter describes the various methods that "invalidators" have in their arsenal, including:

- Keeping the victim in a constant state of uncertainty.

- Projections: taking one's own feelings and projecting them onto another in a negative way.

- Generalizations: exaggerating small truths.

- Judgment: some negative attribute the invalidator attaches to you.

- Manipulation: bad control.

- Sneak attack: "I don't want to upset you, but…"

- Double messages: where the intent doesn't match the words.

- Cutting communication: cutting you off before you finish answering, implying that your thoughts aren't deemed worth hearing.

- Building you up, then cutting you down.

- The double bind: damned if you do; damned if you don't— the lose-lose game.

As I looked at my situation involving the colleague, I realized that I was dealing with:

- An invalidator who needs to be right.

- An invalidator who is compelled to control.

- An invalidator skilled in "cutting communication" so effectively that my voice was silenced.

- An invalidator who uses suppressive mechanisms to chop away at my self-esteem; that is, to persistently deny and discount my input to an important discussion.

And I allowed this to happen! So what can I and other victims do?

Dr. Carter provided a host of coping mechanisms:

- Not taking things personally—a secret of anger management.

- Awareness of the bigger picture—maintaining the larger view.

- Not losing one's situational awareness, staying calm, and seeing things for what they are.

Most important, Dr. Carter provides a roadmap to *confront* the person who invalidated you in such a way that you show you know exactly what that person is doing, from the long, look-'em-in-the-eye pause, to asking the invalidator to repeat the invalidation they just did (which exposes their tactic), to telling the truth about what you are feeling, to mirroring the projection.

Dr. Carter notes that you can always tell the truth by looking at your feelings:

- I feel embarrassed.

- I feel angry that you said it that way.

- I feel put on the spot.

- I feel like I'm being cut off and that my input is not valued.

No one can argue with the way you feel, because right or wrong, it is the way you feel. Telling the truth exposes what is happening and can stop the invalidation in its tracks.

Dr. Carter, in *Nasty People*, also asks the reader to realize that...

- The invalidator is a personality—not a person. (Most invalidators are not in their nasty behavior mode all the time!)

- As victims, we have to examine our own experiences, our own reactions, and our own insecurities. We each make our own set of keys to life; we make each notch in each key from those experiences, and experience-based, imbedded defensiveness can surface at odd moments. We can make ourselves vulnerable, allowing the invalidation to happen. (I have to be aware of and responsible for my own insecurities and not play the blame game.)

- Invalidators usually look big but feel small. Paradoxically, they have low self-esteem but large egos.

- Invalidators invalidate when they feel inferior or out of control—whenever their addiction says "feed me more control—more power—more rightness."

The bottom line is that one doesn't have to be a victim of invalidation—it can be unmasked for the manipulation that it is. It is every person's duty to learn to recognize and divert or defuse the behavioral attack that devalues.

I found the right way to handle my "invalidator." Believe me, he's never tried that again!

Thanks, Dr. Carter. Lights On!

What is Resilience?

When life hands you a lemon, and you find a way to make lemonade…that's resilience!

When you've failed miserably, and you have to find a way to face both yourself and the world again, and you do…that's resilience!

When you are "in a low" and yet you cope in such a way "to find a way to climb through"…that's resilience!

There was a long-term (longitudinal) study conducted a number of years ago in Hawaii, with a control group of at-risk youngsters. These were kids who were in circumstances that on the surface would tend to indicate a very low chance of successfully moving into adulthood as responsible, honorable citizens. And many did not fulfill what was deemed as "becoming successful adults." But of those who did succeed, the ones who overcame the odds, which were clearly stacked against them, shared one important factor. That one factor was that *somebody cared about them.* Somebody cared enough to give them guidance, to smile and affirm their self-worth, to encourage them, to provide a model for them, to lift them up, to pull them forward, to exhibit the value of personal responsibility, to extend a sense of hopefulness for the future. Think about this. Think about how just your smile, just an affirmation, just a word of encouragement can assist a person with their internal coping mechanism, with their ability to be resilient.

Experts tell us that *resilient people develop hardy attitudes and hardy coping skills.* Here are some suggested coping strategies that combine to create resilience:

- Commitment: the willingness to stay involved with people and events throughout a time of change or difficulty rather than pulling back into isolation (persistence/stick-to-itiveness). Do you give up? Or do you see things through? Can you see the path forward?

- Control: working to influence positively much of what happens to you (being proactive). Are you waiting for life to happen to you? Or are you making your life happen?

- Challenge: embracing your experiences, positive or negative, as grist for the mill and a chance to learn and grow (adaptability/forward movement).

When I think of *resilience,* I'm reminded of the opening line in M. Scott Peck's book, *The Road Less Traveled:* "Life is difficult." Thus, we have to be able to cope. And when we can cope with life, we're resilient!

Recommended reading: Salvatore Maddi is co-author of a great book called Resilience at Work and in Life: How to Succeed No Matter What Life Throws at You.

Two more great books for understanding and developing resilience are Stephen Covey's The 7 Habits of Highly Effective People, *and M. Scott Peck's* The Road Less Traveled.

Do You Know What Rejection Feels Like? Can You Rise Above It?

Have you been left off the invitation list? Have you ever been picked last for a team? Do you know the pain of exclusion? Rejection? Have you been passed over for something you really wanted? A column in a popular magazine addressed the spiraling-down emotion that equates with rejection. It is an emotion with which everyone seems to be able to connect. Everyone knows rejection hurts and now science has determined why.

The same brain centers that are activated by physical pain also light up when you experience that social rejection—that *sense of being dumped*. The article "Headache, Heartache: The Pain's the Same" (www.Health.com, 2011) notes that we seem to be hardwired to be hurt by rejection. Even our language connects the physical and the emotional pain, as in "that hurt me so deeply." Ahhh...yet the good news is that once the part of the brain that responds to emotional distress is activated, another part tends to jump in and come to the rescue. It soothes that hurt—and this easing-of-the-pain balm is interestingly connected to emotional language patterns. Yes, our language, our words—the mind aspect connected to words.

The article surmised that this may very well be the best reason yet for writing down your feelings—to help you (using words) to deal with your pain. The power of the personal diary! The power of the gratitude journal! The power of deliberately climbing back up the ladder of emotions by finding and verbalizing higher and more positive ways to describe something good in the situation. Grandma's wisdom that "things will look better in the morning, dear, when the sun can shine on something good in it" holds a deep truth.

Revelation: That "pain" we feel from social rejections is very real; so are our ways for dealing with it and bouncing back! We've got an internal coping safeguard helping us to rise above the emotional hurts. Who says we need to reach for a chocolate bar? There's power in the pen! Lights On!

Gossip...Yuck! Here We Go Again!

As children, we played the "gossip game." We all sat in a circle and someone whispered a sentence in one person's ear. That person, in turn, whispered it to another; this continued until the secret whisper went full circle. The final person in the circle then revealed it. Everyone always laughed at the dramatic change from start to finish. There were lessons that emerged from the game—that words get distorted as each person filters it, and that gossip, at its core, cannot be heralded as truth.

Who cares? You do—especially when the gossip is about you. If you've been the brunt of the rumor-mill at work, of other's opinions that negatively target you, of personal harassment, of undue criticism, of unfairness accentuated through a grapevine, or of e-mail malice, you know that hard-swallowing, deep-in-the-gut hurt feeling.

Sometimes your mind can play tricks on you. You can begin to doubt yourself and your truth. Your response may be that of being offended, insulted, embarrassed, even appalled, or sensing loss or erosion of a reputation, an image, or your personal self-worth. There may be a secret wondering (like in the gossip game) whether there is a truth hidden therein—one that you may or may not want to face. Or the words may hold no truth, and yet your mind, for whatever reasons, takes it in as something negative about you or your behavior. Then you wallow in the negative. Churning can continue for days. Or you may be able to rise above it quickly, discern what you need to, and move on—or not.

I attended a conference where I met a young woman (about 25) who exhibited characteristics of hiding herself. I could not help but wonder what it might be within her story that ran so deeply.

Each day of the conference she wore a different hat. Each hat had a brim that hung over her long bangs; her face was further hidden with big hair. When she spoke, she covered part of her face with her hand. The impression that formed was that she was hiding herself. Was she trying to convey that she wanted to be "out of sight"? If so, why? She was smart, young, articulate, good-looking, and slim, with a great smile and straight, white teeth. I wondered if somewhere along her journey, had she taken in an untruth and that her response was to then hide from the world. (Although I'm not a psychologist, I wondered about whether abuse perhaps had been part of her background.) I simply noticed her outward appearance and the behavior she continually exhibited.

How many times have we taken in criticism that was or wasn't true and wanted to run away and hide from the world? What do you do when you're the brunt of an untruth? What do you do when your character has been assassinated? What do you do when you're unfairly criticized at work or undermined by those you thought were your friends? What do you believe about the situation and yourself? How do you respond?

What if we just stopped in those times and asked ourselves what the situation really is? And then examined whether it is true or not true, and how we know it is true or not true. How we view our situations, our life stressors, is important—because our response differs depending on the beliefs *we* hold about them (not the beliefs that others hold). Therein is the crucial difference. This wisdom gem is huge: *"It is not what happens to us in life, but rather how we respond to it that matters most."*

Recommended reading and study: Byron Katie, founder of "The Work," has one job: to teach people how to end their own suffering. She has a powerful process of inquiry she calls "The Work" and she helps people find that their stressful beliefs (true or not)—about life, other people, or themselves—can radically shift and their lives can change forever. She asks those important questions: What is True? What is not True? How do you react when you think it is true, and how do you react when you know it is not true? She has a process of inquiry to end the internal suffering that goes on inside our minds that is not reality. Her process has a turnaround quotient that can move you forward, ending the story that may have you bound. This is helpful information for our lives, and runs the gamut from the gossip train to that injury which is harbored deeply.

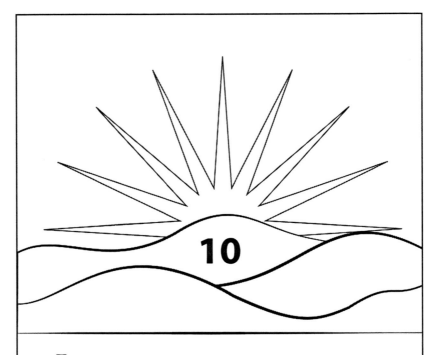

LEADERSHIP FOR WOMEN LEADERS

Distractions That Keep Us from Focusing on Our Goals

(Note from the author: This article is longer than the other articles in this book. Yet this story of the interview with the CEO has much information for women leaders reading this—there are gems of wisdom to glean.)

"If you chase two rabbits, both will get away!"
~Old Chinese Proverb

I supported three female students in a Women's Studies program as they interviewed the CEO of a large firm on the subject of gender equity. One line of questioning was about the small number of women in the higher-echelon positions of his company, and specifically, the "why" of this disparity.

His answer was summed up in one word—*distractions*. He went on to share that, in his view, women (primarily) have many distractions that hinder them from putting full focus on achieving their work goals. And in his particular business, focus is extremely important. He added that these distractions, whether due to societal norms, or individual circumstances, or something else, are not, in his judgment, something negative—but rather that they "just are." He further shared that while distractions are not unique to the female gender, how we work through them tends to differ. He bluntly shared that when we allow everything to become our priority, we then live according to the proverb—we're chasing too many rabbits! And that impacts our effectiveness.

To make his point, he then asked that the audience, comprised of all women, write down on a sheet of paper the one thing they were worried about today, the one thing, major or trivial, that was on their mind in the morning, and that was still weighing on their mind when they entered this room for this afternoon's event. The audience was asked to be fully honest in their sharing. The individual answers reflected a range of concerns such as these:

- Whether her latchkey children would be okay after school.

- Whether a late afternoon conflict resolution meeting would spill over into her planned supper hour with her teen children and husband, and how she would maneuver through that maze.

- Whether or not she'd have time to make a good dinner tonight.

- Whether or not her mother, in a nursing home, was doing okay.

- Whether or not her suit at the cleaners would be ready— because she had a big presentation tomorrow and would she have adequate time to pick it up before the dry cleaning store closed for the day.

- Whether or not her son's teacher would call her tonight about his report card and continued school difficulties. She was also wondering what was really going on in her son's school life.

- Whether she needed to stop for milk, bread, or gas on the way home.

- Whether the prescription for her daughter was refillable, or whether she'd have to call the physician's office and arrange for an appointment before refilling.

- Whether her husband would be able to attend their son's basketball game tonight, and if not, how she would shuffle things to be there for it.

- Whether the anniversary plans for her parent's 50th wedding anniversary would work out as she'd hoped this weekend. There were a variety of obstacles for which she was harboring concern.

The CEO then shared that though it may seem callous, he does not have these types of concerns on his mind, and, admittedly, there are several reasons for that.

First, he schedules brief time periods into his calendar to deal with the daily calls he needs to make for personal matters, to determine what is needed—be it appointments, follow-ups, or getting affirmative information on the types of things the women had noted. He stated that he is not immune from family, household, and related concerns. But he doesn't carry around the worry during the day, rather, he attends to it quickly (within his schedule), and then moves forward with the business goals on which he's focused. He prioritizes what is most important over and over again throughout the day. He underscored that he builds time into his schedule to focus on resolving those distractions, and he does it quickly; he doesn't allow them to linger.

Second, he credits his wife, who shares the effort with him for dealing with their family or household distractions. They have an important and valued partnership for which he is hugely grateful. He also noted that this partnership is key and told the women in the audience that finding and enlisting organized support (friends/relatives) for their work-life-family endeavors is important—continually trying to be "superwoman" keeps you chasing rabbits.

Next, he reiterated that his focus is seldom distracted from the goals he has before him for very long. He shared again, that in his business, and in order to succeed, *undistracted focus on goals is essential.* That means being able to deal with the distractions that do occur quickly and then to get refocused quickly.

A silence came over the group and I could sense that some women—who were single moms—were playing very different scenarios in their minds. I then asked, "Given the societal norms that lift up an expectation for multitasking women, given the nurturing nature of the female species, given that the responsibility role of Mom and Daughter are ever-present, and, given the desire for women to compete in the workplace for higher positions, what is your advice? What is the one thing that you believe women must know and/or do better? Perhaps you can expound on the one thing that, in your view, is holding women back?"

The CEO then shared that he has three daughters, all of whom are remarkable, high-achieving young women. He also shared that his wife, who is his soulmate and helpmate, is also employed full-time outside of the home, doing what she loves—helping others within the nursing profession. He noted that he and his wife and their daughters each have the same 24 hours in a day as everyone else in the room to manage their lives. "How we choose to manage our lives" is the key. Focus is important for business…and also for life! Those 24 hours that we each have to spend need to be focused on what really matters!

He explained further that he and his wife together have taught their daughters the primary importance of having goals. *Goals… goals…goals…goals…goals…goals!*

Setting goals requires you to take the time to *pre-think!* Goal-setting is a deliberate action; it is *not* winging it! It only takes a few minutes, but it does take forethought. It takes thinking about goals every day. Then, achieving those goals takes focus. *It is that focus on goals that allows you to be able to handle life's distractions quickly.* He then asked the audience these types of penetrating questions:

- What was your goal for attending this interview session? What were you expecting to learn? What did you hope to achieve? What do you expect to do with the information you glean from this? How will you incorporate what you've learned today in tomorrow's goals?

- What is your main goal for the balance of this day? What are you trying yet to accomplish? With whom do you need to speak? And what is the goal of that conversation? What do you need to explore? What do you need to decide?

- What is your goal list for tomorrow? What do you absolutely need to accomplish? To complete? To learn? To share? When will you do that?

- In examining your goal for this evening's activities, what pre-thought would have been most beneficial? Who can you ask for support going forward? How can you arrange things differently for a smoother combining of work and home life? What is your goal for assisting your children to succeed in life?

- What does the calendar look like for next week? How does your calendar reflect your roles as mother, daughter, cheerleader? How does your calendar reflect certain times to call the doctor, call the plumber, arrange for a school meeting, or check on your mother in the nursing home? How do you ensure that you are doing the best you can to have order in your life? What are the important goals for next week…for your own self, for your work achievements, for your family life? What matters most?

- What are your real goals for your career? What do you need to learn today to establish your tomorrow? What do you need to be able to do to best contribute to your employer's expectations of you? How will you know you are successful? What steps will you take? When will you take them?

- What is your goal for being part of this Women's Studies Program? What do you expect to glean? What will completing this program prepare you to do? What will be your next long-term goal? If you are job hunting, what is your ultimate goal? Do you have a goal? Or are you settling for whatever happens to happen?

- Are you giving each day the pre-thought that it needs? If not, why not? Are you stopping to prioritize and reprioritize as needed throughout the day? If not, why not?

This CEO clearly made his points. The knowing sighs of this audience were priceless—this group's collective growth journey had commenced. As a gift to the audience, he provided each attendee with a journal/calendar-type book for personal and professional goal-setting and achievement. Each was appropriately inscribed:

"We are what we repeatedly do. Excellence then is not an act but a habit." ~Aristotle

---

Goals and focus are important. Habitual goal-setting and focus is important. Place emphasis on all goals—life goals, work goals, career goals, calendar-scheduling goals, professional goals, personal goals, family goals, goals for today, tonight, tomorrow, next week, next month, this year, next year. Yes, goals to which we give *pre-thought,* and goals on which we then put our *focus.* Yes, we deal with distractions, but we come right back to refocus and reprioritize because we've already thought it through, and we are working our plan!

Lights On!

"In the absence of clearly-defined goals, we become strangely loyal to performing daily acts of trivia until ultimately we are enslaved by it." ~Robert Heinlein

---

Postscript: Life has a rhythm, a pattern. Just as there is white space between the written words, just as there are rest notes between the notes of the musical score, so there are pauses between our actions—brief pauses between our goal achievements. So breathe, rest, and rejoice between those achieving moments, then move on to the next goal activity; there is a natural pattern to successful living!

Do What You Said You Were Going to Do!

Every now and then I'm drawn to a phrase that just seems to fit precisely with a challenge that I'm wrestling with—usually in concert with some consulting work—as I try to find *just the right words* to move a group conversation to a higher level.

Larry Winget pops into my mind—he's known as the Pit-Bull of Personal Development. He is the author of several books and blogs and is a prominent speaker. He is known for "telling it like it is." He doesn't mess around. Something he said seemed to hit the mark as I wrestled with how to get right to the heart of the matter with a group of women who are assigned to the same work group and can't seem to get along, women who are so selfish that they've become blind to the reason they're employed. They are a group of people who feign niceness while undermining the other; who promise cooperation, collaboration, and attention to deadlines in their words, yet whose behavior tells a different story. Have you a similar workplace situation, where people have forgotten why they are employed? And who've forgotten why respectful interpersonal behaviors are key to success?

These are the right words:

- Do what you said you were going to do, when you said you were going to do it, exactly in the way you said you were going to do it.

- Deliver what you said you would deliver, precisely when you said you would deliver it, and in the way you said you would deliver it.

- Call when you said you would call.

- Follow up when you said you would follow up.

- If you can't play nice in this sandbox, then leave—go somewhere else. This sandbox is only for *authentic team players*. That's Business Basics 101.

Are these not the principles that underscore *integrity and trust*?

How is it that so many of our workplaces and work groups seem to have gone mushy, no longer expecting these basic competencies of acting with honor and character? Why are so many of our leaders too timid to "tell it like it is" and to command honesty, follow-through, and basic respect from their employees? Where are the leaders who need to insist that employees deliver on these basics? And to insist that every employee "plays nice in the workplace sandbox."

Tom Peters, co-author of *In Search of Excellence,* said it best: "There is no such thing as a minor lapse in integrity." Leaders set the expectation and then they hold people accountable to act with integrity.

Lights On!

Elephant in the Room[1]

The expression, "elephant in the room" is an English idiom for an obvious truth that is being ignored or goes unaddressed. The expression also applies to an obvious problem or risk no one wants to discuss.

It is based on the idea that an elephant in a room would be impossible to overlook. So people in the room who pretend the elephant is not there have made a choice. They are choosing to concern themselves with smaller and/or irrelevant issues rather than deal with the looming *big* one.

Can you relate? Is your business environment one in which people continue to skirt or ignore the real issues? Do issues linger and fester? Is your particular organization or your work team being trampled by these elephants? Do you believe that (collectively) you are not being the best that you can be? Do you sense how much more effective your organization or work team could be if the people in it could just have better harmony and civility? To all be moving forward together?

Sometimes the elephants in the room can reach the point that people dread going to work—yet no one knows how to call the Big Elephant Game. Rather than acknowledge their elephants in the room, people clearly start up the blame game and behave poorly; it goes round and round and round, and it is ugly.

---

1   *Sometimes the elephant in the room is referred to as the dead elephant, the stinky elephant in the room, the sleeping elephant, or the elephant hiding under the rug. It matters not by what name "it" is labeled. We all know what the presence of an elephant means. Trouble!*

It doesn't have to be that way. Your organization or work team doesn't have to continually be trampled in a heavy elephant atmosphere. You can come out from under the elephants! You don't have to keep feeding them.

While it takes some courage, you, too, can lift up the elephants! Once the elephants are lifted up and all can see them, then they can be appropriately addressed. And then teams and organizations can move forward effectively. Lights On!

Elephants in the Boardroom and the Back Room

An "elephant in the boardroom and in the back room" is something big, real, and impossible to ignore, but often people pretend it is not there because to talk about it could be painful or unsafe. Often we will *not* name our elephants even though they may be crushing us. At Lights On!, we use a proprietary process to lift up those elephants so they can be safely addressed, and the organization can move forward with gusto. (These so-called elephants are the "undiscussables" of an organization that actually cripple it from being the best that it could be.)

Some Examples:

- Repetitive pattern of tardiness and late starts for meetings (creating the need for recaps, and frustrating those who are on time).

- Over-politeness—inability to interrogate reality—not wanting to hurt anyone's feelings. This relates to turf battles, egos, communication blockages, mushroom principle, etc.

- Recycling of issues (lack of accountability, followup).

- Bottlenecks in the organization: overdependence on one or two people in the organization with people unwilling to step forward and take responsibility to get things done that they know need to be done. The pattern is waiting to be told, waiting for direction, and lack of initiative.

- Inability to tell the truth—-where only good news is acceptable or rewarded.

- Mixed messages in the organization.

- Inability of leaders to expect employees to "act with integrity" and to hold them accountable to "do what they said they were going to do."

- Unprofessional behaviors (backbiting, gossip, undermining).

- The *real reason* things are said in hushed tones around the water cooler at the break, but not in the meeting room. That's the initial clue that an elephant is present!

In my work, I've found elephants in the boardroom and in the back room. They are hiding in organizations—nonprofits, for-profits, and municipalities. They hide at the board level, staff level, and team level. They're spoken of in hushed tones around the water cooler and in the ladies' room. They are uncovered when leaders decide to lift themselves from whatever is keeping the organization from being the best it can be. Are you ready to face the elephants in your organization?

Here is a recent testimonial quote from the Regional Director of a Women's nonprofit organization: "The work Claire did with our organization was important because it made us take a close look at some sad truths about ourselves. We faced them, we made the changes required, and we are once more on track."

March Madness

My husband is an avid basketball fan—especially at March Madness Basketball Tournament time. I tend not to get excited about it until the Final Four is reduced to the Terrific Two teams that compete for the championship. Sometimes (en route to the Final Four) there are Cinderella teams whose basketball prowess comes as a surprise. They shine when many counted them out. Who could have predicted that unique team with that special spark would emerge to move forward together so remarkably?

Generally, I avoid sports team examples. But March is different. It's worth making the connection to the world of work and the work team—that's the team of people with whom you share common work goals, interact, and, hopefully, with whom you stay collectively motivated toward the goals! The way a team plays together as a whole determines its success. Well-functioning teams can outproduce the sum of what each individual could do on his/her own. How's your team's performance? Does it have a Cinderella story? Is your work team in an upward spiral? Or not?

Much research has been done on why some teams succeed and why others fail. I think you already know the reasons. I've worked with many work teams and groups and governing boards. So often the team loses sight of the goal because of interpersonal difficulties, egos, conflicts, and elephants in the room that are keeping them from being the best they can be. That can be maddening! But it doesn't have to be that way. The elephants can be lifted up and addressed and the madness stopped…if you want it to be stopped.

Lights On!

Snark-Infested Workplaces

Over the years, my coaching and consulting has provided me with opportunities to work with many people, in many organizations—small and large, for-profit and not-for-profit, white collar and blue collar—and with people across generational lines. Each organization is trying to make sense of things, to move forward with success. Often, there are one or two people who are difficult and challenging in their interpersonal relationships, and that wreaks havoc on the organization. In past years, supervisors would take courses specifically addressing "How to Work with Difficult People." And in most situations, things improved. There has also been the issue of the existence of a few "nasty" people in the workplace—these are people who hurt, betray, or degrade others. They feed on a co-worker's self-esteem, mental anguish, and unhappiness; they like the power that provides. Mostly, nasty people will do their victimizing in a sneaky manner, under wraps, enjoying the cloak of secrecy. Still, the numbers of the "nasty types" were few in the past, and the reputations of the nasty types ultimately tended to do *them* dishonor.

Many of today's organizations present a whole new level in determining who's wearing sheep's clothing and how to deal effectively with extremely manipulative, sarcastic, and hurtful people. There's even a new word to describe this toxic cloud in workplaces. The numbers aren't just a few anymore. It's rampant—that is, *it is rampant where organizations and their leaders have allowed it to remain undetected and to go unchallenged.* That's precisely what gives that behavior power. It's called *snark.*

Snarkers are those who underhandedly undermine, use, abuse, harass, and flat-out *snark* you at every turn. Generation Y people

179

use the term *snarky people*. Some, who think it is funny, refer to *snarking* as an ego-boosting game played by those skilled in delivering and escalating snide remarks. Snarky people prey on those who are weaker. *Snark* is a portmanteau (one word created by the blending of two others) of *snide remark. Snarking* is an adult form of bullying. At its root, it is unprincipled, unkind, disrespectful, and even ruthless behavior—manifesting in snide comments, personal insults, degradations, humiliations, put-downs, jabs, and dissing. ("It's all the same beast," per David Denby of the *New Yorker*, and author of *Snark*.) But it is even more than that—it is a manipulative process of victimization and abuse. It is *invalidation*. It's done by *invalidators*—people who enjoy destroying another's capability to feel happiness, even for just a few moments.

As Jay Carter notes in his book, *Nasty People: How to Stop Being Hurt by Them without Stooping to Their Level*, "if invalidation didn't work, nobody would do it."

Snarking can be stopped in a workplace. (Repeat: Snarking can be stopped in a workplace.) Snarky people can be called out. It is a behavior—a harassing behavior—and harassment of any type is unacceptable. If the leaders of the organization want it to be stopped, they have the situational power to detect it, to openly condemn it, to insist upon and to enforce non-harassing, non-snarking behaviors. To me, it is not a generational thing, nor is it a new thing. Having a workplace that is free of harassment and free of snarking simply makes good business sense—grounded in humane treatment of people principles and in setting an atmosphere for people to be increasingly productive. That's what effective leaders do. That's what effective Human Resource Managers are called to do. Lights On!

The Ides of March: Cynicism in the Workplace

The "Ides of March are upon you" is one of those phrases that is often lifted up as we turn the calendar page to the month of March. It is a negative phrase and one that is steeped in Roman history:

> On his way to the Theater of Pompey (where he would be assassinated), Caesar saw a seer who had foretold that harm would come to him not later than the Ides of March. (Meaning the middle of the month.) Caesar joked, "Well, the Ides of March have come," to which the seer replied, "Ay, they have come, but they are not gone." This meeting is famously dramatized in William Shakespeare's play *Julius Caesar*, when Caesar is warned to "beware of the Ides of March." (Excerpt from a current Wikipedia entry for "Ides of March.")

Our world is a lot different than Caesar's—thank goodness. Still, we have things of which to be wary. We know when things at work, for example, aren't coherent, when cooperation is lacking, when backbiting and belittling behaviors happen, when conflicts run high. We know when there is no congruence; we know when the various arms of the organization are not in synch.

Have your ever felt that your workplace was downright dysfunctional? Or caught yourself dreading to go to work? Or listened to your internal complaint conversation with yourself as you drove home? Likened to the Ides of March, is modern-day cynicism closing in on you? Maybe that airline commercial jingle, "Wanna get away?" is enticing to you right now.

The good news is that it doesn't have to be that way! Dysfunctional can become functional. Incoherent can become coherent. Uncooperative can become cooperative. Negative can become positive. Conflicts can be resolved. Teams can become professional, including yours. There's a choice. Which do you choose? It takes good leadership, strong principles, clear expectations, accountability, followthrough, and the means to all be rowing together in the same direction, pursuing shared goals because you want to! Goodbye, cynicism! Hello, enthusiasm! Lights On!

Why Are Our Work Relationships so Difficult for Us?

In my consulting work in Business Leadership and Effectiveness, I continue to run into the same type of human relations issues that I did in my former life as an HR manager. People just seem to get "tangled up." Emotions take hold, egos puff up, and rational thinking is blurred. That's not a good recipe for making progress.

Simply being human—with thoughts, passions, needs, wants, egos, defensiveness, and habitual behaviors, complicates the mix. Most times we're trying to resolve conflict with only half-truths, or lack objectivity or clarity on what is real. What are the facts? Then add the important business factors—the necessity for *change*, the need for increased productivity, the need to be more competitive, the need to move forward with gusto, the need to streamline, update, do things decidedly differently, and, yes, to improve—and the entire mess gets very complex. Tension mounts as opposing forces increase. Unfortunately, there is no one-size-fits-all recipe for resolution!

Michael Grinder, noted author and expert in nonverbal behaviors, shares that "the epicenter for all conflict is in rights/perceived rights." These are also known as *needs*. To get to a point of resolution for these conflicts won't happen until those alleged *rights* or *needs* have been excavated...often very carefully as in an archaeological dig. Once lifted up and given voice, only then can movement proceed towards resolution—opening a pathway to creative problem-solving. These conversations are difficult; it is so important to stay on the high road and engage purposefully.

That's where principles of expected behavior come into play and why having standards of conduct are so important. All need to be clear that constructive behaviors are paramount.

Of equal importance is having clear intentions of where the business is headed, and why, and what collectively is needed to reach the business goals. The importance of having clear, well-communicated, and well-understood rules and workplace goals must be underscored. All in the workplace need that clarity and focus for coherence and alignment to move forward together. It is a process.

Conflicts are an opportunity for growth. When you are able to resolve conflict in a relationship, it builds trust. Other good can stem from conflict. Conflict produces change, it can lead to unity, and it can promote collaboration. Remember, *peace is not the absence of conflict...but the ability to engage purposefully with conflict.*

The summer 2011 edition of *Spirituality and Health* magazine was devoted to relationships of all kinds. One poignant question was posed by the editor. To really get underneath the tangle of a difficult relationship, ask: "Why is it that he/she or we/they cannot *choose* peace?" (Perhaps that is the root question to ask of all workplace relationship entanglements.)

Postscript: In any moment, peace is a choice. Is it for you? Lights On!

Me, Myself, and I–And Now Us—A Living System Organization

Who hasn't sung with a child that fun, yet deeply true, song that goes, "Oh, your head bone's connected to your neck bone, and your neck bone's connected to your shoulder bone?" The lyrics continue all the way down to your toes and back up and around again.

Over time, the illustration expands from just a song into a deep sense that our personal being is connected in body, mind, and spirit. Each of us is a whole living system, and within our individual living systems, numerous processes are doing their work almost unnoticed, e.g., digestion, respiration, circulation, as well as endocrine and nerve functions. Each process is part of the vital, complex interconnectedness.

Living Systems

Living systems have the distinction of being able to adapt to changes in their environment. Complex chemical and neurological communication systems provide feedback, each to the other. As living systems, we consciously learn from and reflect upon our experiences. We can visualize possibilities for the future and then prepare for them. We communicate in many ways, and, because we are social, we can communicate through conversation. We each have a sense of who we are, of our relationships with others and with the external world. We learn, we grow, we change, we adapt, we co-create, and we seek coherence through patterns and processes. We continually sense that the environment is capable of transformation. We have capacities for inquiring, finding and trying solutions, reflecting, learning, and growing. Our being, without even realizing it, is self-organizing all the time. And we are not alone. We are connected to everyone and to everything else.

185

The Living System Organization

An organization is like a pliable, porous container with an inside and an outside. It is constantly in motion, constantly integrating complex and dynamic relationships. Without people, and without people relating to other people, an organization would obviously not exist. It is made up of people who are living, working, and relating in a particular environment; they are capable of transformative change, much like a living system.

Ask yourself the following questions about your organization as a living system. Examine it for congruency and coherence.

- Is it healthy?

- Is it adaptable to change?

- Are feedback and communication open and flowing?

- Is learning and relearning taking place?

- Is it growing? Is it progressive?

- Has it visualized the future and prepared for it?

- Is the organization clear on its identity, purpose, and intentions?

- Is there clarity and coherence among the functions of its parts?

- Is there cognition of existing patterns and processes?

- Are underlying issues addressed?

- Are differing views invited, discussed and measured against clear principles? Are they synchronized to advance the purpose and goals of the organization?

- Is quality conversation across the board encouraged?

- Do members know what is going on and why?

- Are new ideas supported, encouraged, and integrated?

- Do the leaders lead with integrity and clarity?

- Do the ground rules for interacting together support the organization's intentions? Are they principle-based? Are there clear and simple rules?

Analyzing organizations as if they were living systems is important. Congruence, or lack of congruence, is often very visible. Organizations that are congruent, or that exude coherence and clarity, are generally more effective, sustainable, and healthy. Those that have adopted the above principles are usually better at addressing their problems, challenges, and issues and are more successful at prioritizing the most important things. Such organizations succeed because their members understand what is (or is not) happening within the interconnections. Their leaders are skilled at uncovering and addressing hidden problems while supporting the organization's development and evolution.

Extraordinary results are achieved when organizations embrace the idea that they are living systems—mindful of connections, exhibiting clear intentions, rewarding collaborative effort, being caring and relational, remaining open to honest conversation, sharing information, and adhering to principle-based and collectively enforced accountability standards.

Is your organization a living system?

Note: This Article was written by Claire Knowles and published in Washington Woman Magazine *in February, 2005. It is reprinted here with permission.*

Organizational Sensing and Assessment

What is organizational sensing? It is a deep-level evaluation that makes what is happening "under the surface" of the organization, team, or workgroup visible to the leaders of an organization. Once the issues are lifted up, constructive changes can be advanced. Ask yourself the following questions:

- Do you know what the under-the-surface issues are that may cripple your organization or block it from achieving world-class performance?

- Do you know what the "undiscussables" are that result in misalignment, rework, blaming, complaining, mediocre performance, recurring problems, and productivity losses?

- Do you know what the patterns and processes are that run deep within your organization? Both the positive patterns that can be enhanced, and the negative patterns that can be changed? The patterns that impact productivity? Safety? Quality? Effectiveness? Alignment? Overall performance?

- Can you identify three simple rules that play out over and over again and that impact your organizational or team success? Or conversely, can you identify rules that impact organizational or team difficulties?

These can be lifted up. If you want to make things better, these can be made visible so that they can be constructively addressed for the future.

Coaching for groups and organizations is important for targeted growth and development. If you are in a group that is stuck or where progress is slow, understanding where the group stands (sensing/assessments) and being able to see the potential of what might be possible (turning on the lights) is paramount. There are many coaches in many domains ready to assist this forward movement. Most coaches have certifications and have a variety of tools and modalities to offer. Why not choose growth and a targeted path to success?

Leaders: consider the iceberg. You see only what is on top. Yet it is the hidden, under-the-surface issues that need to be made visible so that your organization or team can markedly advance forward.

Coaching

Why would a person call a coach?

As a personal, life, executive, and organizational/team coach, I am often asked to explain *specifically what do I coach*—beyond the general terms of coaching reference career concerns or about facing and embracing a life transition. Recently, this has been the nature of my personal coaching. Individuals have requested coaching because of:

- An inability to set boundaries and stick to them.

- The repetition of (negative) life or career patterns, including the inability to see them or to take the action to break the patterns.

- The inability to voice one's concerns or to be proactive toward making a change that has to be made.

- Feeling disconnected—needing a subtle nudge to move forward.

- Needing help to name the issue so that it can be lifted up and addressed.

- Developing inner courage to address some particularly difficult workplace issues.

Why would a team or organization call a coach?

Teams and organizations sometimes "get stuck."

Sometimes they become dysfunctional. Sometimes it is because they lose track of what is important and cannot see the forest for the trees. Sometimes they actually know that the health of their team or organization is failing; they are not making the progress they'd hoped to achieve. They need someone to help them clarify their work goals and to develop the principles to live by and to lead by, so that their interactions and their conversations are geared to meeting and exceeding their respective work goals. Sometimes teams and organizations need a coach to help them to be able to identify and deal with the "undiscussables"...the very things that are preventing them from moving forward. Once brought into the light, the undiscussables become discussables. Ahh...the power of being able to name something for what it is and then starting the important conversations about it... conversations that transform!

Sometimes teams just need some frameworks and models to use to move them forward. Sometimes it is necessary to "get real" and to lift up for an organization what is going on...as seen from the coach's viewpoint. Sometimes leaders in organizations need some help in assessing the options and alternatives.

Good, reputable coaches recognize the importance of human connectivity and leadership (in organizations, and in one's personal life). Coaches know that constructive human connectivity is one of the last frontiers for exponential growth— the place where teams and organizations can realize a new and sustainable competitive edge quickly. That's vital to the success of your business, team, or organization.

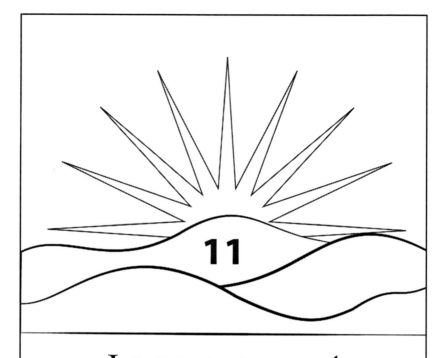

11

Lights on!
Little Bursts
of Light

"We do not remember days…we remember moments."
~Cesare Pavese

"A reminder that our lives are comprised *not* of calendar days, months, and years, but rather of moments of life's unplanned magnificence. The encounters, incidents, mix-ups, hassles, honest mistakes, triumphs and difficulties, near misses, dalliances, high points, low points, dilemmas and predicaments that we go through *are* our lives—and not just what happens along the way *to* our lives! *Cherish the Moments! Enjoy the Journey!*" ~Author unknown

"Conscious Living depends on finding out what goals are important to you, staying focused on them, and moving toward those goals at a pace that allows you to feel vibrant.

What would you be doing if you were living at your full-out best? If you knew you could not fail, what would you do differently? What is it that is calling you?

It is possible to make rapid shifts in consciousness—from scarcity to abundance, from defensiveness to openness, from fear to love—and these shifts in consciousness will change the outer circumstances of your life. You can choose to become the source of attitudes such as gratitude and responsibility (rather than waiting for the events of life to move you to adopt them)."
~Gay Hendricks, PhD (*A Year of Living Consciously*)

"To change your life: start immediately, do it flamboyantly, no exceptions." ~William James

"Your life today is a result of your thinking yesterday. Your life tomorrow will be determined by what you think today." ~John C. Maxwell

"Seek out that particular mental attitude which makes you feel most deeply and vitally alive, along with which comes the inner voice which says, 'This is the real me.'"
~William James

"Have you been keeping your Gratitude Journal? Here's a good reason why to do that! Appreciation is the antidote to fear. It is the purest, strongest form of love. Research now shows that it is physiologically impossible to be in a state of appreciation and a state of fear at the same time. Appreciation is the first and most fundamental happiness tool." ~Dan Baker, PhD, and Cameron Stauth (*What Happy People Know*, Rodale)

Accepting Criticism with Grace…Age-old wisdom teaches that whenever someone criticizes something you have done or criticizes you personally, you should do three things:

1. Stop and listen intently to the criticism, as our critics can be our best teachers.

2. Decide what part of the criticism is *constructive,* and accept what you might learn or do differently with the clear intent to make things better.

3. Decide what part of the criticism is *destructive* and *let it go*—spend no further time and invest no more energy in revisiting it!

"What is truth? A difficult question, but I have solved it for myself by saying that it is what the voice within tells me."
~Mahatma Gandhi

"What is following my bliss? The realization of your bliss, your true being, comes when you have put aside the so-called requirements of life that you should live this way, or that way. Follow your bliss…where the deep sense of being is from and where your body and soul want and are drawn to go. When you have that feeling, then stay with it and don't let anyone throw you off. Don't be afraid to follow your bliss and doors will open where you didn't know they were going to be." ~Joseph Campbell

Intuitive insights: What kind of signs/feeling do you get or watch for when something isn't right for you? Contracting energy? Confusion? Energy drop? Sense of distancing? Repelling? Disengaging? What kind of sign/feeling do you get or watch for when something is right for you—when you intuitively know you need to proceed? Welcoming; with ease; drawn to; sense of knowing; clarity, rightness, certainty; compelling forward movement? We have the ability to receive intuitive guidance. Are you listening? Are you paying attention?

Accept compliments: Research shows that being able to recognize your positive qualities and accept compliments (simply saying "thank you" the next time a co-worker admires your new outfit) can boost self-esteem—as opposed to whisking those compliments away. Proponents of positive thinking note that giving yourself a pep talk—and accepting the kind words of others—when you're feeling stressed or blue can actually counteract those negative emotions and improve your mood. Lights On!

TESTIMONIALS

"I've been to workshops covering things like this before, but never have I seen it all come together like this."

—AK, The Synergy Group & Triple Track HR Partners,
Williamsville, NY

"I would recommend this annually! I think it is important to take a break from the routine and rediscover yourself. Claire, you're an outstanding workshop leader, whose warmth and caring nature made us open up very easily. Thank you."

—RL, Workshop participant in a Lights On! Workshop for Personal
& Professional Path-finding

"The work Claire did with our Zonta organization was important because it made us take a close look at some sad truths about our club operations. We made the changes required and are once more on track."

—PR, Zonta Club, Niagara Falls, NY

"Dear Claire, just wanted to tell you once again how grateful we are for the time you spent with us today preparing the roadmap to help us make Zonta the club it was meant to be. I will do my best to help make this a reality. Thanks again for all your time and expertise spent so lavishly on us today."

—DW, Zonta Club, Niagara Falls, NY

"Claire—I want to say how much I enjoyed our session on Thursday. It renewed my energy and appreciation for working here at this place, at this time and with these people. I especially liked the range of topics you can use to get your point across; from fun to dead serious... on the topic of discussing personal issues with each other. You are a terrific trainer! Onward!"

—NG, Staff Leadership Interaction,
Wellspring House, MA

"There is great value in your presentation, and in your work with us because of your ability to work with an Executive Director and a Board President to assess the real needs; and your ability to tailor the workshop to the group and even adjust throughout the workshop. You kept everyone engaged and on task. I think everyone was surprised that the day went by so quickly and they were left wanting more and were inspired to move forward together. You helped us get focused on a larger picture with strategic plans and visions. You brought great energy and enthusiasm to the group and made them aware of how important their work is. Thank you, Claire."

—JT, Effectiveness Workshop,
Tonawanda, NY - YWCA

"Claire Knowles helped us to express and clarify our deepest reality, engaging board, staff, program participants and volunteers in the conversations. The process wasn't easy; it disturbed some settled ideas, challenged us to experiment and discover; it revealed a healthy and leader-full organization, able to take us on its future work with confidence."

—NS, Former Executive Director,
Wellspring House, MA

"Claire... I enjoy work again and I have hope! As far as organization, you lifted us up to another level. The level of professionalism, respect and teamwork has increased; the progress is remarkable. You woke our employees up! You made them aware of inappropriate negative behavior; their behaviors have been modified positively. The elephants were brought out into the open. The focus on serving our clientele has been underscored. You gave us steps to keep focused on these issues on an on-going basis. For your potential clients: If you feel that chaos (games, lack of teamwork, poor communication, unprofessional behavior) occurs too often with your employees, there is hope for a better, more humane workplace. Trust Claire... She knows what she's doing!"

—Private Firm, Niagara Falls, NY

Claire Knowles, *Consulting, Coaching, Facilitation, Presentations, Retreats.*

Creator of Lights On! Workshop© in association with R.N. Knowles & Associates, Inc.

E-mail: Claire@ LightsOnLeadershipSuccess4Women.com (or) CEFK1@aol.com

Cell: 716-622-7753

Websites: www.LightsOnLeadershipSuccess4Women.com www.LightsOnWorkshop.com www.RNKnowlesAssociates.com

Leadership doesn't just happen... It emerges...!

We help people (teams and organizations) to teach rational solutions to complex problems while simultaneously building the social connections and emotional energy and commitment to quickly and effectively get the best results. If you want your team, organization, or business to move forward quickly and achieve your key initiatives—with clarity, coherence, and collaborative success, please call us at **716-622-7753.**

Professional, business-focused, effectiveness-raising, result-oriented process... so your team, group, or organization moves forward with focus and deliberateness:

- Principle-based, superior performance
- Proprietary models
- Coherence-building
- Problem-solving
- Path-finding
- Clarity of intentions & actions
- Clear roadmap to follow
- Deep learning
- Lifing up the group's potential

...All in one day and using a simple process that brings it all together.

Lights On! and Lights On! Workshop© are especially for women: Success Workshops, Speaking Engagements, Retreats, Facilitations, Presentations, Coaching, and Consulting for women-run businesses and women's organizations. Lights On! was created by Claire Knowles in association with Richard N. Knowles & Associates, Inc.

PRAISE FOR THIS BOOK

"You will absolutely love this book. Claire has a beautiful way of dressing up life's lessons with thought-provoking metaphors. She writes with clarity and enjoyment and shares her deep wisdom. Claire is one of these people that you rarely meet who can touch your soul with truth. Through her storytelling, she invites you to remember to always keep your *lights on* and do your life with ease."

—Marilyn Segal
Life Purpose Blueprints
Spiritual Teacher/Healer
Author of *The Heart Speaks...Creating Your Own Heaven on Earth*
and co-author of *Whose Illness is it Anyway?* with her twin sister,
Carolyn Cohen

"Claire Knowles is a wonderfully experienced facilitator and motivator. With warm-hearted stories, clear council, and many years of experience she shares her wisdom in her book and sheds 'lights on' many areas helping us to grow and become more of what we can be. This book is a little treasure to read and to share."

—Gunilla Norris
Author of a series of books on hearthside spirituality, including:
Being Home, Becoming Bread, Inviting Silence, A Mystic Garden and
Simple Ways

"With a gentle touch, Claire Knowles allows life to teach her, and by extension all of us. Would that we all could adopt the ways she learns the lessons of life, from everything that occurs around her. As women, we can, and we deserve to, pay attention to her accessible wisdom, and accept her invitation to 'turn our own lights on'!"

—Martha Johnson, MEd.
Author, Clarity Coach, Blogger,
Author of *Why Not Do What You Love?, Musing Along the Way*
www.TakeTimeForYou.net

"Storytelling is an ancient tradition that helps us make sense of complex situations in our lives. Like Aesop's Fables, Jataka's Tales, or the Panchatantra, Claire Knowles' delightful and insightful tales help us to reflect on our and others' perspectives of life, and how those perspectives impact what we do in life and our relationships with others. Her tales illustrate how our perspectives impact our quality of life, as well.

Sometimes it is difficult in today's complex, ever-changing world to recognize the dynamics in which you find yourself. Claire's wonderful 'Lights On!' series helps one to reflect and see the dynamics at play, helping us to not only be better leaders, but better people through the process."

—Beverly Gay McCarter
Principal, Human Mosaic Systems, LLC
www.HumanMosaicSystems.com

"There is something remarkably comforting in the way Claire weaves her personal experiences and beliefs into simple but profound lessons for the rest of us to take away. Perhaps its her word choice, experience crafting stories or innate wisdom. Whatever it is, her spirit spoke to me as I read one insightful gem after another. What a wonderful gift she's given us! Here's to your possibilities!"

—Sara Russell
President & Founder, Feel the Possibilities
A Division of Sarandipity, LLC

"This book will inspire you to look for the positive light within yourself! It is like the author, Claire Knowles, is your personal confidante and is sharing her daily insights. Her writing encourages you to challenge the negative focus of the world and instead look for the positive. Claire's unique career experiences in the work world shine through as she lights a path for women to continue to move forward professionally and personally."

—Cathi Brese Doebler
Author of *Ditch the Joneses*

"Life is in the small moments, but they can be easily overlooked in our busy lives. Claire Knowles' reflections shine a light on those little moments in life, revealing them to be really the big moments in our lives."

—Birute Regine
Author of *Iron Butterflies:*
Women Transforming Themselves and the World

"Whether it is a pair of shoes or clouds that resemble mashed potatoes, there is a life lesson to be noted. Claire shares these life lessons through her words. Her articles help the reader to find the positive in every situation. Claire clearly and beautifully lifts this up—*Life is a stream of choices and we each control our destiny.*"

—Laura Ward
Eckerd College, St. Petersburg, FL

"Over the years Claire's inspirational articles and seminars have made me re-evaluate many aspects of my personal life and business. I have learned to handle business situations with clients and employees in a way that allows everyone to move forward in a positive direction. She has given me that 'push' to make needed changes to balance my life. Every article makes me stop and reflect on my own life. So I am extremely pleased that this *Lights On!* compendium has been developed into book form, shareable with many people."

—Renee Cerullo
President, RLComputing
President, NYS Women Inc., Buffalo Niagara Chapter

"In working with Claire in several of her Effectiveness Workshops, I've admired her skill in asking penetrating questions, with poignancy and a keen ability to get to the heart of the matter. She engages a disciplined process that creates a powerful trajectory in moving organizations forward toward achieving their goals. This book, *Lights On!*, offers the same type of questioning approach—shedding light on our situations, revealing deeper truths, enabling us to see the opportunities before us, and illuminating the path forward—with a positive bent that is both encouraging and energizing."

—Patty Brown
Co-Founder, Integrated Business Ventures, Inc.

"Truly Inspirational! Through *Lights On!* you have an opportunity to define your journey and see the spark that lights your life. Claire Knowles' stories compel you forward, helping you to shine, to clarify your own path, and bring joy to your own seeking."

—Nydia Santiago, PhD
Health & Wellness Coach
Clearwater, FL

"When the inspiration of words can powerfully enlighten our hearts, our souls, and our minds, merging together in sheer harmony to create the sort of wisdom that emerges in light, we then know that its author has touched our lives in a way that may benefit our days on this earth. *Lights On!* inspires in such a way, thanks to the loving wisdom of author Claire Knowles."

—Dori Montini-Kotzin
President, Western New York Women
www.WNYWomen.com

CPSIA information can be obtained at www.ICGtesting.com
Printed in the USA
BVOW071613041012

302175BV00002B/7/P